The era of the Second World War

Contents

Oxford University Press 1993

Oxford University Press,
Walton Street, Oxford OX2 6DP

*Oxford New York Toronto
Delhi Bombay Calcutta Madras
Karachi Kuala Lumpur Singapore
Hong Kong Tokyo Nairobi
Dar es Salaam Cape Town
Melbourne Auckland Madrid*

and associated companies in
Berlin Ibadan

Oxford is a trademark of
Oxford University Press

© Oxford University Press 1993

ISBN 0 19 917 211 0

Typeset by MS Filmsetting Limited,
Frome, Somerset.
Printed in Italy by
G. Canale & C. S.p.A. - TURIN

⚏ Preface

This book follows the premise of the others in this OUP series. It is structured as an investigation into two key questions about the period: **Why did the Second World War not break out before September 1939** and **Could the Axis Powers have won the War**? In the introductions to the first two sections of the book, which develop these themes, students are asked to put forward and record an initial hypothesis, using their existing ideas, assumptions, and the sources provided in the introductions. As students work their way through the material in the book they can use the evidence which they will find to confirm or amend their hypotheses. In this way they will gain some understanding of the historian's method and of the notion that historical judgements are often provisional and subject to change in the light of new evidence.

Most, but not all, of the exercises are focused on the various Attainment Targets and these are identified according to the convention explained in the *Notes to Teachers*. Other exercises test comprehension and the ability to make inferences from the text.

Neil DeMarco

⚏ Notes to teachers

Exercises providing opportunities for developing students' understanding of the concepts and skills required in the Attainment Targets are signposted below. In each of these exercises there is a specific question which sets out to test the AT covered by the exercise. These questions are indicated by an *asterisk*. The other questions in the exercise can therefore be seen as 'unpacking' or stepped questions with an incline of difficulty, leading towards the specific question. The questions with asterisks also have mark schemes which are to be found in Teacher's Resource Book 2.

AT1a Changes 27, 53, 62, 66
AT1b Causes and Consequences 12, 21, 32, 41
AT1c People in the Past 13, 38
AT2 Different Views 20, 30, 36, 47
AT3 Evidence 8, 15, 34

INVESTIGATING THE SECOND WORLD WAR

⊯ History: 'One damn thing after another'?

Henry Ford once complained that history was just 'one damn thing after another'. I suppose he meant that history seemed to be nothing more than a long list of facts and events, piling up endlessly, one after another, without any idea of a pattern or link between them. Perhaps, as you come to the end of Key Stage Three history, you are beginning to agree with him.

History used to be taught like that. Pupils had to learn long lists of 'important' dates, the names of the kings and queens of England and famous battles. Now pupils are encouraged to think for themselves in history and to try to use the same methods and approaches as historians.

This book will encourage you to use one technique adopted by historians: *hypothesis formation*. I started this textbook with two basic questions about the era of the Second World War:

⊗ *Why did the Second World War not break out before September 1939?*
⊗ *Could the Axis powers (Germany, Italy, and Japan) have won the Second World War?*

Henry Ford's view of history

These questions are looked at in the following chapters. Obviously, I knew something about the war before writing this textbook so I had some *hypotheses* (theories) about these questions to begin with. All historians begin with hypotheses which require hard evidence to back them up. Sometimes the historians will find that the evidence does not support the hypothesis they started with. In that case, they have to change it to reflect the evidence. The cartoon below shows how the process works.

B Why did the Second World War not break out *before* September 1939?

Ein Volk, ein Reich, ein Führer!

Hitler skilfully exploited the need of the German people for leadership and pride in their country

This introduction provides you with a range of sources which should help you to develop an hypothesis of your own about why the war did not break out before September 1939. Remember, an hypothesis is only a rough answer and it is quite acceptable to change it or improve on it later. You may be wondering why I am not asking the more obvious question: 'Why did war break out in September 1939?' rather than 'Why did it not break out *earlier*?'

First of all, by answering the question why was there not a war *before* September 1939, you end up with the answer to the question 'Why did war break out in September 1939' anyway. By trying to explain why something in the past did *not* happen, you get a better understanding of why something else did happen.

Secondly, this type of approach – called 'counter-factual' thinking – helps to get across the idea that some causes are more important than others. For example, Hitler behaved aggressively from the moment he came to power in Germany in 1933. He could have provoked a war in 1936 and twice in 1938. But war did not happen – so German aggression alone cannot explain the reason for war in 1939. There has to be *at least one other reason to explain it.*

Hypothesis grid: Why did war not break out before September 1939?		
Possible reasons	**Effects**	**Evidence**
1 The First World War	The First World War caused so many deaths that people would do anything to avoid another war.	
2 The Treaty of Versailles	The Germans felt unfairly punished by this treaty and wanted to see it torn up.	The Germans resented the massive cuts in their armed forces – only 100,000 soldiers in their army which was now very weak.
3 Pro-peace attitudes in Britain		
4 The attitudes of the World powers to Hitler		
5 Hitler's secret plan, 1936		
6 Rearmament in the 1930s		During 1939 Britain and France built more planes than Germany for the first time since 1933. Therefore, they were more ready for war now.
7 The German invasion of Poland		Hitler's invasion of Poland did lead to the outbreak of war with Britain and France but he was not expecting them to fight over Poland.

≣ Hypothesis grid

On page 4 there is a hypothesis grid which you should copy out into your book or file and then fill in as you work through the relevant chapters (1–3).

Most of the following sources (A–G) suggest possible reasons why the war did not break out before September 1939. Study them carefully and answer the questions on page 6. When there is no specific question about a source, think what the source may be providing in the way of evidence for the investigation.

After you have studied the seven sources and answered the questions, fill in your copy of the hypothesis grid. Under each heading in the 'Effects' column, give your view of what each of the sources says about why the war did not break out before September 1939. For example, after reading Source A you could write: 'The First World War

caused so many deaths that people would do anything to avoid another war.' What this means, therefore, is that politicians and the public in general would try very hard to avoid another war with Germany until there was really no other alternative. In September 1939 Hitler invaded Poland – a country Britain and France had promised to help. When this happened, there was no alternative to war with Germany.

As you work through chapters two and three, your task is to find evidence which supports (or goes against) your hypothesis about the outbreak of war in 1939. In each section of the grid you can indicate the page numbers where you have located some relevant evidence and outline what the evidence says. The first two effects have already been filled in and three of the evidence columns have also been partly filled in for you.

Source A

Some of the figures for soldiers killed in action in the First World War.

Great Britain and Empire	947,000
France	1,360,000
Germany	1,800,000
Italy	615,000

Source B
The Treaty of Versailles

The treaty which Germany was forced to sign at the end of the First World War in 1919 contained several terms which many Germans found humiliating:

- Germany was to have an army no bigger than 100,000 men.
- The Germans were not allowed to have any tanks, submarines or military aircraft in the armed forces.
- Germany lost 13 per cent of her territory to other countries.
- Germany had to pay £6000 million in gold to Britain and France as compensation for starting the war.

Source C

A peace demonstration in Britain in the 1930s

Source D

This cartoon was published in Britain just after the Germans marched into the Rhineland – something they were forbidden to do by the Treaty of Versailles. It shows the attitude of the other major world powers to Hitler. The figure at the front of the group on the left is Eden, the British Foreign Secretary.

Source E

Hitler's secret order, 1936
I therefore lay down the following task:

a   The German army must be ready for combat in four years.
b   The German economy must be capable of war in four years.

Source F: Rearmament – numbers of military and civilian aircraft built each year

	1933	1934	1935	1936	1937	1938	1939
France	600	600	785	890	743	1382	3163
Great Britain	633	740	1140	1877	2153	2827	7940
Germany	368	1968	3183	5112	5606	5235	8295

Source G

The Germans invade Poland, September 1939

FORMING YOUR OWN HYPOTHESIS

1   Source B suggests reasons why the Germans were very bitter about the treaty. But does it help to answer the question why did the war not break out before 1939?

2   What does Source C suggest about the attitude in Britain to a possible war with Germany?

3   How does Source D help to explain why the countries of Europe avoided war with Germany?

4   Does Source E help to explain why war did not break out before 1939? Explain your answer.

5   Do the statistics in Source F help to explain why Britain and France wanted to avoid war with Germany before 1939? Explain your answer.

THE LEGACY OF THE FIRST WORLD WAR

✳ The traditional explanation for the outbreak of war in 1939

The standard or traditional explanation for the outbreak of the Second World War has concentrated on the role of Hitler as the man responsible for causing the war. It takes as its starting point the Treaty of Versailles which ended the First World War. The standard view goes something like this:

'The Germans felt humiliated and unfairly punished by the Treaty of Versailles. Adolf Hitler used this sense of anger to launch his National Socialist Party to power in Germany in 1933. During the next six years Hitler built up the German war machine with the intention of creating an empire in the heart of Europe. Hitler knew that, eventually, he would have to go to war with Britain and France to create this empire. The democratic powers*, Britain and France, tried all they could to avoid war, but eventually realised that only war would stop the monstrous evil Hitler represented. When Hitler invaded Poland in September 1939, the British and French governments realised that the time for war had arrived.'

German youth was a key target of Nazi propaganda. Why do you think the Nazis were so keen to win the support of students?

German graves at Langemarck First World War cemetery in 1940. Was their sacrifice in vain, Hitler would later ask?

This view has been challenged in more recent years by historians who have shifted the focus away from Hitler and Germany towards world political and economic factors. These will be discussed in chapter 3.

It is helpful, in the meantime, to look more closely at the effects of the First World War on the people of Europe. This will help you to understand why people opposed the idea of another war so strongly.

Some of the 8 million men on all sides who did not return

ASSOCIATION OF EX-SERVICE CIVIL SERVANTS

FIT FOR HEROES

NO WORK
NO MONEY
NO FOOD

YET Men and Women of
INDEPENDENT MEANS
WORK IN 6 DEPARTMENTS

A FITTING WAR MEMORIAL

HUNDREDS OF
DISABLED MEN
DISCHARGED BY THE GOVERNMENT

HUNDREDS OF
CONSCIENTIOUS OBJECTORS
IN BRITAIN

A GRAVE SCANDAL

An unemployed disabled ex serviceman in 1921.

* PACIFIST

Someone opposed to the use of war or violence to solve disputes between countries

✳ The legacy of the First World War

The effects of the terms of the Treaty of Versailles on Germany have already been looked at in Chapter One. They *were* harsh and there is no doubt that the Germans felt both humiliated and unfairly treated. Hitler provided them with the chance to regain their self respect.

The war had other consequences or legacies in addition to the bitterness of the Germans. Altogether, over eight million soldiers lost their lives and there was a real determination that this war should have been the 'war to end all wars'. There was anger because the war seemed to have been fought for no worthwhile cause. The men who returned from the trenches, many of them mutilated, faced a life without the dignity of work and were dependent on an inadequate pension. They felt cheated. They had been told they were fighting for 'King and Country' and were promised a 'land fit for heroes' on their return. Instead, they quickly found themselves out of work and the promised homes remained just that – promises.

Pacifism

During the 1920s many Britons came to believe that war could no longer be justified. They believed that if the leaders of nations behaved sensibly they could always find a peaceful solution to every crisis. These pacifists* were especially active during the 1930s and in 1936 they set up the Peace Pledge Union. Its members swore to take no part in any future war.

Source A

Why cannot our children be taught that the seeds of the Second World War were well and truly sown in that Treaty and although there was a twenty year period of germination the bloody harvest of the Second World War was inevitable? Why not explain that the vengeful [punishing] Treaty of Versailles provided very fertile ground for the madman Hitler to brainwash the German people with his war-like Nazi philosophy ...?

(W.H.A. Groom, *Poor Bloody Infantry*)

Herbert Read fought in the First World War. In 1940, after the Second World War had begun, he wrote another poem to the men who were once again off to France to fight another war against Germany:

Source B

We went where you are going, into the rain and the mud;
We fought as you will fight
With death and darkness and despair;
We gave what you will give – our brains and our blood.

We think we gave in vain. The world was not renewed ...
... Our victory was our defeat.

(Herbert Read, *To a Conscript of 1940*)

Source C

More than anything I hated to see war crippled men standing in the gutter selling matches. We had been promised a land fit for heroes; it took a hero to live in it. I'd never fight for my country again.

(Private W.A. Turner quoted in M. Middlebrook, *The First Day on the Somme*, 1971)

EVIDENCE: THE LEGACY OF THE FIRST WORLD WAR

1 Which of these sources supports the view that
   a the First World War led directly to the Second World War?
   b the First World War was not worth fighting?
   Quote extracts from each of the sources to back up your answers.

2 What evidence from the text that you have read so far could be used to support the views of W.H.A. Groom (Source A)?

3 What do you think Herbert Read (Source B) meant by the phrase 'Our victory was our defeat'?

4 What evidence could you use from the text to explain the attitude of Private Turner in Source C?

5* Which *one* of these three sources is most helpful in explaining why there was so much opposition in Britain to another war? Give reasons for your answer.

✳ Europe 1815–1919

As we have seen, many accounts of the causes of the Second World War have focused on the role of Hitler. Clearly, he did play a major role. After all, the troops who invaded Poland in September 1939 were German and this sparked off the war. The problem with concentrating on Hitler is that other less obvious reasons get overlooked.

Some of these reasons go back to before the First World War. Others involve events several thousand kilometres away from Europe in the Far East. Understanding these causes helps us to be able to answer the question asked in Chapter One: *Why did the war not break out before September 1939?* It will be helpful to look at the causes of the First World War since some of them are also relevant to the Second World War.

Britain's world-wide empire in 1900 seemed threatened by Germany

Causes of the First World War: Europe 1815–1914

During the hundred years between 1815 and 1914 there was no large-scale war in Europe. The major European powers tried to keep the peace by co-operating in what was called the *Concert of Europe* ('Concert' meaning union or league). Through the Concert, the major powers of Europe would settle any disputes peacefully. The Concert also tried to make sure that no single, continental European state became so powerful that it could dominate the others.

Britain was happy with this balance of power* because she was the world's most powerful country and wanted to keep things the way they were. Although Britain was obviously a part of Europe, she was more concerned with events outside Europe and maintaining her world-wide empire.

> *** BALANCE OF POWER**
>
> A situation in which the major countries of a region are all roughly equal in power

Pre-First World War Europe, showing the system of alliances

The German 'threat'

In the last 25 years of the nineteenth century a new, strong nation emerged in the centre of Europe: Germany. She had no intention of maintaining the balance of power in which all the major states of continental Europe were roughly equal. She intended to become the dominant continental power and this worried Britain.

Britain joined two other states in Europe who also felt threatened by Germany: France and Russia. Germany also found an ally — the Austrian Empire. Each side frantically built up its armed forces to prepare for war. When war did break out in 1914, it was welcomed with tremendous enthusiasm by the people of these countries, all convinced that their cause was just.

THE ARRIVAL OF GERMANY AS A GREAT POWER

1. Explain the meaning of the term 'balance of power'.
2. Explain the meaning of the term 'Concert of Europe'.
3. Why do you think Britain was so keen on this 'Concert' of European powers?
4. Why did Germany become dissatisfied with the policies of the 'Concert'?
5. Why did Britain, France and Russia object to Germany's aims?
6. Do you think Britain, France and Russia had done anything to avoid war with Germany before 1914?

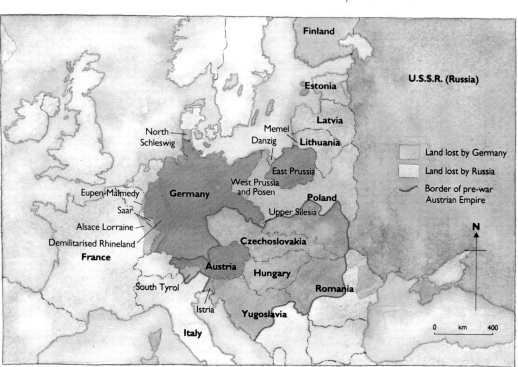

Europe after the Treaties of Versailles and St Germain, 1919

EUROPE BEFORE AND AFTER THE FIRST WORLD WAR

1. Which *completely new* states were set up in 1919 that were not part of Europe before the war?
2. Which countries lost land as a result of the war?
3. Which three countries lost land to make up the state of Poland?
4. Of the countries which lost land, why might Russia be considered as the odd-man-out?
5. How do these maps help to explain why many Germans felt angry about the treaties which ended the First World War?

Why was there not a war in the 1920s?

Europe in the 1920s

After the First World War the major European powers — except Russia and Germany — set up the League of Nations. Its purpose was to keep the peace in the world and so prevent another war like that of 1914–18. The nations of the world would work together through the League to settle disputes between nations peacefully.

The Treaty of Versailles was forced on Germany to make sure she would never again be powerful enough to threaten the balance of power in Europe. Germany was excluded from the League, and the United States and Russia did not join.

During the 1920s the authority of the League of Nations was not challenged by Germany. This picture shows a League of Nations meeting in 1926.

German prosperity

In the 1920s Germany's economy and military strength were too weak to challenge the power of Britain and France. But during the 1930s she was once again in a position to try to become the dominant power on the continent of Europe.

Before Hitler came to power in 1933, Germany was a democracy and its government was generally prepared to keep to the terms of the treaty. There were no other major countries in Europe prepared to try to overturn the treaty and defy the League of Nations. So even if the Germans had wanted to challenge the treaty and the League, no other powers would have been willing to help them. In addition, Britain and France were still recognised as powerful states and they were generally in agreement about what needed to be done to maintain the peace in Europe.

Besides, as the decade progressed, most Germans became less angry about the treaty and the defeat in the war. The 1920s were mostly a decade of prosperity for Europe. The German economy, boosted by American money, was very prosperous between 1924 and 1929. The average German had little reason to worry about the Treaty of Versailles while life was treating him so well.

Does growing German prosperity in the 1920s help to explain the fall in support for the Nazi Party?

Election results for National Socialist Party	
1924 (May)	32 MPs
1924 (Dec)	14 MPs
1928	12 MPs

Total number of MPs in parliament: 480

1* Which of the reasons on the left do you think was the most important in leading Germany to keep to the terms of the treaty? Explain your answer.

On page 11 four reasons were given why Germany did not make a serious attempt to overturn the Treaty of Versailles and defy the League of Nations in the 1920s:

- Germany did not have a powerful enough military force.
- Germany was a democracy and was prepared to co-operate with Britain and France in keeping to the treaty.
- Germany was prosperous during most of the 1920s and therefore the defeat in the war and the treaty were less of a problem.
- No other major European power was willing to challenge the treaty and the League of Nations.

You can sometimes come to a decision over difficult questions like this, involving causes, with the following technique. If you can remove one of the reasons given above and still end up with the same result (Germany not attempting to overturn the Treaty of Versailles) then you have a less important cause. If, for example, you believe that even if there had been another country willing to help Germany challenge the terms of the treaty, she would still not have done so, then this reason could not have been that important.

✳ Conclusion

There is not much material in this chapter to explain why the war broke out exactly when it did – this will come in the next chapter. But if you think carefully about the sources above you should find enough evidence to suggest why the idea of war was resisted so strongly – at least in Britain and France. How does this help to explain when the war began?

This chapter has also discussed a number of reasons which explain why war did not break out in the 1920s. Some of these reasons will be of help in filling in your hypothesis grid.

The next chapter concentrates on events in the 1930s. You will soon realise that some of the reasons which helped to keep the peace in the 1920s did not apply to the 1930s, and this made war much more likely.

In the 1930s the Germans were joined by Japan and Italy. All three powers were ready to defy the League of Nations. The peace of Europe and the world would be fatally weakened.

Japan defies the League of Nations. This cartoon was published in 1932 and shows Japan treating the League of Nations as a doormat.

The rising sun – the symbol of the new, emerging power of Japan in the Far East

The Fasces (centre) – symbol of authority and power in Ancient Rome. It was adopted by Mussolini as the symbol of Fascist Italy.

WHY DID WAR NOT BREAK OUT UNTIL 1939?

⩕ Europe in the 1930s: the decade of dictators

There were many changes in Europe during the 1930s. For one thing, in 1929 a depression* struck the world and its effects — bankruptcies, unemployment, homelessness and despair — were felt particularly strongly in Germany. Germans lost patience with their democratic government which had failed to bring them prosperity and turned to the government offered by Hitler, which became a dictatorship*. His promise to tear up the terms of the Treaty of Versailles and establish Germany once again as the dominant power on the continent of Europe had tremendous appeal. Hitler came to power in 1933, just as the Depression was coming to an end. Hitler's economic policies helped to speed up the return to prosperity.

By 1933 two other powers, Italy and Japan, also had reasons to challenge the balance of power and the League of Nations. They formed an alliance with Germany. Japan had ambitions to dominate the Pacific, and Italy wanted an empire in Africa. Germany planned an empire in the heart of Europe. As in 1914, Britain and France were again faced with the problem of halting the expansion of Germany and they made the same decision. On 3 September 1939 Britain and France declared war on Germany after Hitler's invasion of Poland. This time, though, the people of Britain, France and Germany remembered all too clearly the suffering of the First World War and there were no scenes of enthusiasm for war — just acceptance.

> *** DEPRESSION**
> A situation with little economic activity, high unemployment and falling living standards as people become poorer

> *** DICTATORSHIP**
> A system of government in which one leader has total power over the country

PEOPLE IN THE PAST: THE ORIGINS OF THE TWO WORLD WARS

1 Study the text on this page and in chapter 2 comparing the origins of the two world wars and then copy and fill in the chart below.

2* In what ways were the reasons for war in 1914 and in 1939 similar and in what ways were they different?

	Before the First World War	Before the Second World War
Was Britain anxious to maintain the balance of power before both wars?	Yes/No because . . .	Yes/No because . . .
Was there a system of international co-operation to maintain the peace?	Yes/No because . . .	Yes/No because . . .
Was this system challenged by Germany?	Yes/No because . . .	Yes/No because . . .
Was the conflict concerned mainly with Europe?	Yes/No because . . .	Yes/No because . . .
Was the war welcomed by the public of the major powers?	Yes/No because . . .	Yes/No because . . .

The Nazis skilfully used the disillusion with the democratic government to boost their popularity in election posters like this. To what sort of Germans would this poster have appealed and why?

Germany's expansion plans. What did these three states (Poland, Austria and Czechoslovakia) have in common?

Hitler's decision to increase Germany's army in 1935 beyond the limit set by the Treaty of Versailles was a challenge to Britain and France. This picture shows a parade of new German tanks at Nuremberg in 1935.

Roosevelt

CONSCRIPTED ARMY

An army which all fit men of a certain age have to join for a period

The 1930s: war by miscalculation?

There is no doubt that Hitler was determined to break the terms of the Treaty of Versailles, especially those restricting the size of the German army. He planned to re-establish Germany as Europe's dominant power. He would achieve this by moving Germany's borders to bring states like Austria, Czechoslovakia and Poland under direct German rule or influence. However, this does not mean that he *wanted* a general European war –

let alone a *world* war.

Hitler may have wanted a short, limited war in Europe. There is some evidence to suggest that Germany was only capable of fighting a short war in 1939, and Hitler knew this. But this does not explain entirely why a war broke out. Why was Germany able to threaten the peace of Europe in the 1930s but not in the 1920s? What other factors inside and outside Europe contributed to a situation which made war likely?

The United States

The United States played no real role in European politics in the 1930s but her lack of interest in European affairs was an important factor in helping to bring about war. The USA was the most powerful country in the world – just as she is now. She was also a democracy and disliked Hitler's Germany.

Roosevelt, the President of the United States, could have threatened Hitler by promising to join Britain and France if they stood up to Hitler and found themselves at war. In 1935 Hitler announced

that Germany would have a conscripted army* of 500,000. This was a direct attack on the Treaty of Versailles, since Germany was allowed an army of no more than 100,000. Instead of confronting Hitler over conscription, Britain and France let it pass. It was clear to Hitler that neither of these democracies would stand up to him. If the United States, Britain, and France had joined together to enforce the treaty against Germany, Hitler may have backed down once and for all.

Other dictators: Mussolini

There were other dictators* in the world apart from Hitler and they encouraged each other. Mussolini, the dictator of Fascist Italy, showed Hitler how easy it was to defy the League of Nations as well as Britain, France and world opinion. In the same year that Hitler announced the introduction of conscription, Mussolini launched an unprovoked attack on a member of the League of Nations – Abyssinia (now Ethiopia). Mussolini claimed that the backward Abyssinians needed to be civilised by a European power. The 'benefits' of this new 'civilisation' included poison gas and the flame-thrower!

The League urged its members not to trade with Italy. This policy, known as imposing sanctions, made little impression, especially as League members were still allowed to sell oil to Italy. Without oil, the Italian invasion would have ground to a halt within a few months. Hitler offered to supply Italy with any raw materials that she needed, in defiance of the League's policy. Besides, Germany had left the League of Nations in 1934 and had no intention of supporting its policies. As a result, the two dictators grew closer. Mussolini's view of the League was: *'The League is all right when sparrows quarrel, it fails when eagles fall out'*.

CREDERE OBBEDIRE COMBATTERE

Mussolini, like Hitler, was an excellent speaker. Huge crowds hung on his every word, spellbound. Why was the ability to make stirring speeches so important to dictators like Hitler and Mussolini? The words written under Mussolini are 'Believe', 'Obey', and 'Fight'.

> *DICTATOR
>
> Someone with total power to govern as he pleases

Source A

Abyssinia was an easy target, and in 1935 Italian troops easily overran the country. Here was another test for the League, just like the invasion of Manchuria. This time not only was the aggressor condemned but economic sanctions were also passed. Ships were forbidden to carry arms to Italy or take goods away from Italy. But the sanctions proved useless. Above all, Italy's oil supplies were never cut off.

(Harry Mills, *Twentieth Century World History in Focus*, 1984)

Source B

'Oil and argument' – a British cartoon, February 1936, showing Mussolini as the tank's driver

---

EVIDENCE: THE LEAGUE OF NATIONS AND MUSSOLINI

1 Explain why Source A refers to Manchuria as 'another test for the League'. (Read the section 'Other dictators: Hirohito of Japan' on page 16 before answering this.)

2 How does Source B get across the idea that the sanctions against Italy were useless?

3 In what ways do Sources A and B agree about the effects of sanctions?

4* 'The cartoonist in Source B is only expressing his opinion so the cartoon is of little value to the historian.' Explain why you agree or disagree with this view.

Japan's expansion plans

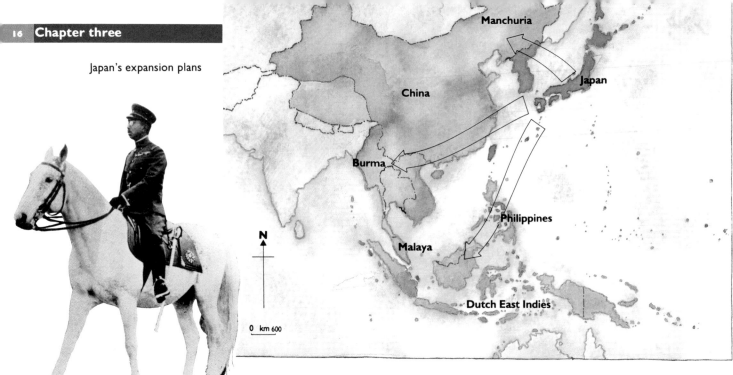

Emperor Hirohito

Japanese troops in China in 1938

Other dictators: Hirohito of Japan

Like Italy and Germany, Japan was a dictatorship, in which only the views of the Emperor Hirohito and his military advisers counted.

Government policy was also dominated by *militarism* – the idea that military might is the best way to achieve your political ambitions. Japan's ambition was to dominate South-East Asia and the South Pacific. By doing this she could acquire all the raw materials she needed to become the region's dominant power.

Japan's invasion of Chinese Manchuria in 1931 was the beginning of this strategy. The League protested about this unprovoked attack on one of its members. Japan left the League and then went on to invade the rest of China in 1937. The United States woke up to the fact that Japan now threatened its role as the dominant power in the Pacific area. War was just four years away.

THE CHALLENGE OF THE DICTATORS

1 Which other powers, apart from Germany, threatened the balance of power in the 1930s? Explain why they were a threat.

2 What evidence is there in the text that Hitler did not want a major European war in the late 1930s?

3 Why was the United States' lack of involvement in European affairs in the 1930s so helpful to Hitler?

4 What do you suppose Mussolini meant by the sentence quoted on page 15? Does the evidence so far support Mussolini's view of the League or not? Explain your answer.

5 Why was Germany in a better position to challenge the authority of Britain and France in the 1930s than she was in the 1920s?

⩘ Europe 1936–39: the slide to war

Hitler's actions between 1936 and 1939 did lead to war in Europe. That is not the same thing as saying that Hitler wanted a war in 1939 or that it could not be avoided. Neither does it mean that Hitler was the only cause of the war. It is quite possible that Hitler did not expect to have to fight a war with Britain and France over Poland. He was probably convinced he could seize Poland without involving other European powers. The next few pages will explain why.

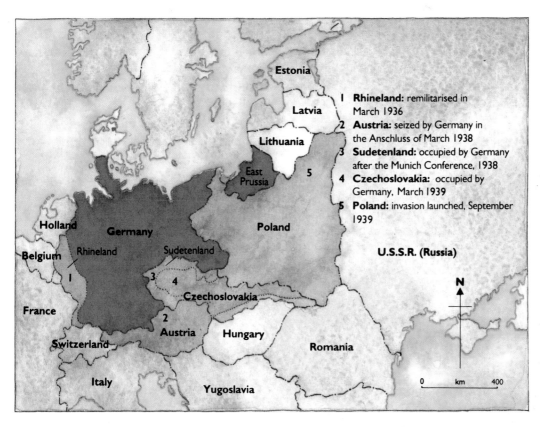

1 **Rhineland:** remilitarised in March 1936
2 **Austria:** seized by Germany in the Anschluss of March 1938
3 **Sudetenland:** occupied by Germany after the Munich Conference, 1938
4 **Czechoslovakia:** occupied by Germany, March 1939
5 **Poland:** invasion launched, September 1939

German expansion in Europe, 1936–39

The Rhineland: the turning point

In March 1936 Hitler ordered German troops into the Rhineland area of Germany. According to the Treaty of Versailles, no troops or military defences were allowed in the Rhineland. France was ready to take a stand over this breach of the treaty and sent troops to the border with Germany. France was prepared to force Hitler to back down if Britain agreed to support her. Britain made it clear that she was not prepared to go to war to keep German troops out of their own territory (the Rhineland). Britain was desperate to avoid war with Germany and, like France, overestimated the size of the German armed forces. France was sure that the German army numbered 295,000 men and that she could not fight them alone. In fact, the German army was nowhere near as powerful as this at this time.

For Hitler, the gamble paid off. The French backed away and Hitler's secret orders to his men to withdraw from the Rhineland, if they were attacked, were never needed. Hitler was convinced that he could achieve what he wanted without a war because Britain and France would never stand up to him.

Timeline 1931–39

Copy the timeline below on the left into your file.
Place the letters representing the events below next to the correct year on the timeline as you read about them in this chapter. One of the events has already been done for you.

A Munich Conference
B Japanese invasion of Manchuria
C German occupation of the Rhineland
D Japanese invasion of China
E German invasion of Poland
F Italian invasion of Abyssinia
G German seizure of Czechoslovakia
H German Anschluss with Austria
I Nazi-Soviet Pact
J Hitler became dictator of Germany

1931 | 1932 | 1933 | 1934 | 1935 | 1936 | 1937 | 1938 | 1939

B

* RAW MATERIALS

Basic substances that are essential for modern industry, such as coal, oil, and various metals like iron ore

Austria, the Sudetenland, Czechoslovakia: more of the same

Encouraged by the easy victory over the Rhineland, Hitler made further plans for expansion, convinced his opponents would never try to stop him. In March 1938 German troops marched into Austria and Hitler declared that from now on Austria was part of the new Germany. This *Anschluss*, or union with Austria, was also forbidden by the Treaty of Versailles. There were protests from the British and French but nothing more.

Six months later, Hitler demanded that the Sudetenland region of Czechoslovakia be handed over to Germany. He claimed that because some three million Germans lived in the region, they had the right to be part of the new German *Reich*, or state. The Sudetenland also contained vital raw materials* and the Czechs' impressive weapons factories. The British Prime Minister, Chamberlain, and Daladier of France agreed to meet Hitler in Munich along with Mussolini to discuss Hitler's demands.

The Munich Conference in September 1938 gave Hitler everything he wanted. The Sudetenland was handed over to Germany. The Czechs were not consulted and neither was the Soviet Union — a country which had an alliance with Czechoslovakia and was prepared to help her. The Czechs were told that they were free to oppose the agreement, but Britain and France made it clear that the Czechs would have to fight Germany on their own. The Czech army of some 35 divisions (about 500,000 men) was modern and well equipped, but it could not fight Hitler on its own.

Hitler promised that he would make no further demands in Europe. Chamberlain returned to Britain and was heartily cheered as a hero and peacemaker. Six months later, in March 1939, German troops seized the *whole* of Czechoslovakia. Chamberlain and Daladier at last realised that the German leader could not be trusted. Both countries signed an alliance with Poland, promising to help the Poles if they were attacked by Germany.

Probably no more than half the people of Austria welcomed the Anschluss with Germany. This picture shows German troops entering Austria in March 1938.

The Nazi-Soviet Pact

Hitler paid no attention to the Anglo-French promise of help to Poland. And who could blame him? The British and French had done nothing to stop the introduction of conscription in 1935, the occupation of the Rhineland or the Anschluss with Austria. They had handed the Sudetenland to him. Why would Poland be any different?

Hitler was much more worried about the response of the Soviet Union. The Russians had tried to negotiate some agreement with the western democracies (Britain and France) to oppose Hitler, but the British and French had not seemed too interested. Stalin, the Soviet dictator, was certain that the West was secretly encouraging Nazi Germany to expand eastwards against the Soviet Union. A war between Communist* Russia and Nazi Germany would go down well with Britain and France. Hitler was concerned that an attack on Poland, without Soviet agreement, might well lead to war with Russia. Hitler wanted a war with Russia but not *then*.

In August 1939 the Soviets and Germans signed the Nazi-Soviet Pact in which they promised not to attack one another. Secretly, they agreed between them to invade and occupy Poland, each taking half the country. Hitler was confident that the one power which might have stood in his way, the Soviet Union, was no longer a problem.

Poland Doomed

The Nazi-Soviet Pact sealed Poland's fate and made war in Europe almost inevitable. The western democracies had a chance to win Soviet support in the mid 1930s to form an alliance against Hitler but, it seems, they hated Communism more than they feared Nazism. The loss of the Soviet Union as a possible ally for Britain

and France made Hitler's task a great deal easier.

Less than a week after the Nazi-Soviet Pact, on 1 September 1939, German troops invaded Poland. Two days later Britain and France stood by their promise to Poland and declared war on Nazi Germany. The Second World War had begun.

This cartoon about the Nazi-Soviet Pact shows Hitler and Stalin in a three-legged race together

Stalin

COMMUNISM

A form of dictatorship in which the government controls industry; in Hitler's dictatorship the government left most of the industries under private ownership

'What next?' Americans were well aware of the danger that Nazism represented. Here Hitler views his next victim from the top of his swastika steamroller. The US refused to become involved in Europe's affairs in the 1930s. But what does this cartoon suggest about the American attitude to Nazi Germany?

Source C

'Nightmare waiting list.' British cartoon on Munich

Munich, 1938

Source D

When I think of those four terrible years [1914–18] and I think of the seven million young men who died, the thirteen million who were maimed and mutilated, then I am bound to say – in war there are no winners, but all are losers. It is those thoughts which have made me feel that it was my duty to make every effort to avoid a repetition of the Great War in Europe.

(Chamberlain's speech (adapted), July 1938)

Source E

I will begin by saying what everybody would like to ignore or forget but which must nevertheless be stated ... we have experienced a total defeat. Silent, mournful, abandoned, broken, Czechoslovakia disappears into the darkness ... You will find that sooner or later Czechoslovakia will be swallowed up in the Nazi regime ... And do not suppose this is the end. This is only the beginning.

(Churchill's speech (adapted) on the Munich Conference)

Source F

Chamberlain gave Hitler everything he asked for. Hundreds of thousands of Czech citizens and the magnificent defences of their frontier were handed over ... It was not only Czechoslovakia that was ruined. We and the French had lost a good cause and our good name; we had lost a well-armed ally on Germany's southern frontier and the chance of resisting Germany in alliance with Russia. We rearmed during this year [1938–39], but not to equal the Czech arms which had been thrown away. Chamberlain did not realise the disaster he had helped to cause.

(E. Nash and A. Newth, *Britain in the Modern World*, 1967)

Source G

The British statesmen [concerning Munich] used practical arguments: the danger from air attack by the Germans if war broke out, the backwardness of Britain's military forces. It would be impossible for Britain to help Czechoslovakia even if she had the military strength. British policy at Munich supported the belief that the Germans were entitled to the Sudetenland on the grounds that it was German territory. The settlement at Munich was a triumph for British policy – not a triumph for Hitler. It was a triumph for all those who believed in equal justice between peoples.

(Adapted from A.J.P. Taylor, *The Origins of the Second World War*, 1961)

Source H

British crowds cheer Chamberlain's return from Munich

DIFFERENT VIEWS: 1938

1 In what way does Source D explain why Chamberlain gave in to Hitler at Munich?

2 What is Churchill's opinion of Chamberlain's actions at Munich?

3 Is the cartoonist in Source C more in agreement with Chamberlain or Churchill? Explain your answer.

4 'Source H clearly shows that Chamberlain's policy was the more popular and this means he was right to do what he did.' Explain why you agree or disagree with this view.

5* Which of Sources C, D, E and H support the view in Source F regarding Munich and which support the view in Source G? Explain your answer.

ADVISING CHAMBERLAIN AT MUNICH

It is easy to look back at Chamberlain's behaviour at Munich and point out the mistakes he made. After all, we know what was to happen twelve months later with the German invasion of Poland. Being able to make use of information not known to people at the time is called 'hindsight', and hindsight makes experts of us all. Your task in this assignment is to write a 300-word report to Chamberlain just before Munich pointing out the pros and cons of agreeing to Hitler's demands and of refusing them. Remember, you can only make use of what was known to the British at that time so you cannot make any precise references to the state of Germany's military strength. On the other hand, you are well aware of Britain's military strength.

CAUSES AND CONSEQUENCES: THE SECOND WORLD WAR

*In the exercise in page 12 you were asked to consider the reasons why Germany was content to go along with the terms of the Treaty of Versailles and not defy the League of Nations in the 1920s. Those reasons are listed in column A of the chart on page 22.

If these factors had still applied during the 1930s, then it is fair to say that the war would probably not have broken out in 1939. Sources I–N below relate to the 1930s. They deal with the same sort of issues as those in column A but they refer to the 1930s. Source N, for example, deals with Italy's challenge to the League of Nations and so is helpful in discussing reason 4 in the chart.

Copy the chart into your file or exercise book. Fill in Columns B and C. Point 3 of Column B has already been done for you but you can change it if you disagree – historians often do! If you believe that by the end of the 1930s the German military was powerful enough to challenge the authority of the League, then say so in the first box in Column B – but you must find some evidence to support this view from the text and the sources below. This *evidence* goes in Column C.

Are any of the points you have made in Column B about why Germany defied the League of Nations more important than others?

Source I: Military strength, 1939

	Soldiers	Combat aircraft	Major ships
Germany	800,000	2,765	11
Britain	220,000	1,144	76
France	800,000	735	21

Source J

In November 1937 Hitler called a meeting of his military chiefs. He outlined his military plans. Colonel Hossbach made these notes of the meeting:

'German politics must reckon with its two most hateful enemies, England and France ... The German question can be solved only by way of force, and this is never without risk ... For the improvement of our military position it must be our first aim ... to conquer Czechoslovakia and Austria.'

Source K

When Japanese troops moved forward to take in all of Northern China ... the world began to take seriously a document written by a Japanese Prime Minister in 1928 and discovered by China in 1931 – the Tanaka Memorial, a huge plan of world conquest going as far as India, Asia and Europe.

(Adapted from David Low, *Years of Wrath*, 1949)

Source M

Per capita income in 1938 (average income per person in dollars per year)	
Germany	$487
Britain	$498
France	$248
Poland	$92
Soviet Union	$188

Source L: German unemployment in millions

1932	1933	1934	1935	1936	1937	1938
5.6m	3.7m	2.3m	2.1m	1.6m	0.9m	0.2m

Source N

Italian troops placing a mountain gun into position in Abyssinia in 1935

Germany and the League of Nations in the 1930s

Column A: **Factors explaining German reluctance to challenge the League of Nations in the 1920s**	Column B: **Your view on whether the reasons in Column A were still relevant during the 1930s**	Column C: **Evidence from Sources I–N and from what you have read in the text so far which supports your answer in Column B**
1 Germany did not have a powerful enough military force in the 1920s to try to challenge the terms of the Treaty of Versailles and the authority of the League.		
2 Germany was a democracy and was prepared to co-operate with Britain and France in keeping to the treaty.		
3 Germany was prosperous during most of the 1920s and so the Germans were less bothered by memories of the treaty because they were doing well.	Germany was increasingly prosperous after the Depression of 1929–32. The evidence of Sources L and M proves this. The Germans were well off in the late 1930s yet then they defied the League and the treaty so it could not have been very important in the 1920s.	
4 No other major European power was willing to join with Germany in challenging the treaty and the League during the 1920s.		

⩘ Conclusion: Why did war not break out before September 1939?

This chapter should have given you several ideas for your hypothesis grid, which should now be complete. How important, for example, was the desire in Britain among the people and political leaders (like Chamberlain) to avoid a war at all costs? Did Hitler really plan the war as early as 1936? How decisive was the Treaty of Versailles in leading Germany to start the war? There is not really a wrong or right answer to an exercise like this but, whatever your view, you must have evidence to support your judgment. Remember, though, the best answers make use of the widest range of sources. You may find, therefore, that an answer which concentrates only on the role of Hitler will end up ignoring a lot of other evidence and historians should never do that — even if pupils sometimes do!

THE WAR IN EUROPE AND NORTH AFRICA 1939–43

⚜ Introduction: Could the Axis powers have won the war?

The central question of chapters 4–6 is:

⚘ *Could the Axis powers (Germany, Italy and Japan) have won the Second World War?*

Once again, there are several sources for you to look at and a hypothesis grid for you to fill in. It is worth remembering that just because something in the past *did* happen, it does not mean it *had to happen*. Sometimes it only needs one event to change in a sequence of events for the outcome to be different.

For example, you might believe that the rise to power of Hitler in the 1930s was inevitable – that it had to happen. We all know that it did happen but could it have been different? In the November 1932 elections in Germany, the Nazi vote fell by two million. Their support was dropping as Germany was recovering from the depression of the early 1930s. What if the German President, Hindenburg, had decided not to make Hitler Chancellor in January 1933? If he had waited just another six months, Nazi support would probably have dropped still further and Hitler's chance might have gone forever. Events might have turned out quite differently.

Setting up your hypothesis

To make it easier to develop your hypothesis, three ideas about the possibility of an Axis victory are given in the grid below. One of the columns already has some evidence filled in for you.

Remember, you shouldn't fill in all of your grid now. Leave space so you can add more evidence from chapters 4–6. You should be able to find more evidence in these chapters which helps to provide an answer to the question: 'Could the Axis powers have won the Second World War'? Sources A–F will give you some ideas of your own to begin with.

An election poster from the 1930s featuring Hitler and Hindenburg

Source A
Money spent on armaments, 1940 (after the surrender of France) The amounts are given in US dollars (in billions) so you can compare the expenditure.

Britain	$3.5
Germany	$6.0
Italy	$1.0

Source B
Money spent on armaments, 1943 (after the surrender of Italy)

Britain	$11.0
Soviet Union	$14.0
United States	$37.5
Germany	$14.0
Japan	$ 4.5

(Paul Kennedy, *The Rise and Fall of the Great Powers*, 1988)

Hypothesis grid: Could the Axis powers have won the Second World War?	
Possible theories	**Evidence in support of/against your hypothesis**
1 The Axis powers (Germany and Italy) could have won the war in 1940.	In the view of *The Spectator* (Source D), only Britain stood in the way of Germany controlling all of Europe. Therefore, Germany must have been close to victory.
2 The Axis powers could still have won the war in 1941.	
3 From 1942 onwards the Axis Powers (Germany, Italy and Japan) had little chance of winning the war.	

Source C

Aircraft production, 1944

Allies	
USA	96,000
Soviet Union	40,000
Britain	26,000
Axis	
Germany	40,000
Japan	28,000

Aircraft were the most important of all weapons of war. Who controlled the skies would win the war.

A German bomber on a raid over London

A Lancaster bomber of 50 Squadron

The Lancaster could carry a bomb load of 4500 kg – twice the heaviest load of any German bomber

Source D

The Battle of Britain – A British view:

This has been described as the most important week in the history of our country . . . It is the day of decision in the sense that if Hitler can break the spirit of this people . . . the last enemy will have gone down before him and control of Europe will be his.

(Adapted from *The Spectator* magazine, September 1940)

Source E

The Battle of Britain – A German general's view in 1945 (interviewed by Liddell Hart):

Our idea was to finish the war as quickly as possible and we *had* to get across the water to do that. There were many preparations in progress, but the weather outlook was not good. The attempt [at invading Britain] was supposed to be carried out in September [1940], but Hitler cancelled all the preparations. The Navy's heart was not in it. Neither was the German Air Force strong enough to stop the British Navy.

(Liddell Hart, *The Other Side of the Hill*, 1951)

Source F

A modern textbook on the German invasion of Russia, June 1941:

Only Britain remained unconquered in Western Europe, and Britain would surely be forced to make peace if the Soviet Union fell . . . At first the Germans were highly successful. In all areas the German panzers [tanks] smashed forward, advancing up to twenty miles [30kms] a day. The Russians, taken by surprise, retreated in the face of superior forces, and the Soviet air force was destroyed on the ground on the first day of the invasion. In the north the Germans reached the outskirts of Leningrad in early September and in the south they took the important city of Kiev.

(Nigel Kelly, *The Second World War*, 1989)

1940 – CLOSE TO DEFEAT?

1 What, according to Source D, would happen if Britain lost the Battle of Britain?

2 Does the general in Source E think Britain came close to defeat in 1940?

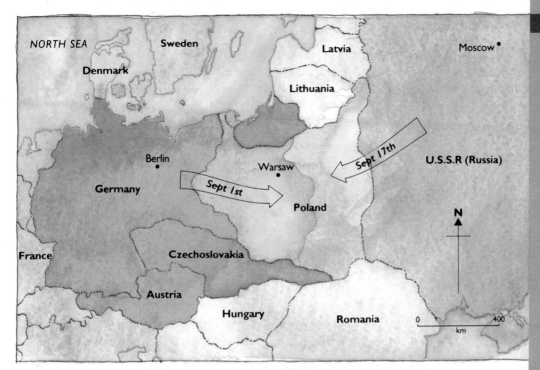

Nazi and Soviet invasions of Poland

⚔ Poland engulfed

The Germans invaded western Poland on 1 September 1939. Two days later, Britain and France declared war on Germany. The Poles were overjoyed, confident that with British and French support the Germans could be beaten. Crowds of happy Poles swarmed around the British and French embassies in Warsaw to express their gratitude to their new allies.

On 17 September, Russian troops invaded eastern Poland, as had been agreed secretly in the pact signed between Hitler and the Russian leader, Stalin, in August. Poland was now faced with two enemies attacking on two fronts. By the end of September, Poland ceased to exist. The Russians took one half of Poland and the Germans the other.

British and French land forces in western Europe had scarcely fired a single shot and had stood by as the Polish state disappeared, even though France alone had 57 divisions on its German border facing just 32 German divisions. (A division, on average, numbered about 15,000 men.) An attack on Germany then, when most of its

German troops advance into Poland

armed forces were involved in Poland, could have achieved remarkable success. But the French lacked the necessary aggressive spirit. By the end of September, the Germans had increased the number of divisions on the French-German border to over 100. The British Royal Air Force, however, did find time to drop 18 million leaflets over German cities, suggesting that Hitler was a bit of a scoundrel.

⚙ Blitzkrieg

The key to Germany's success over Poland and the string of victories that followed over Belgium and France was Blitzkrieg. 'Blitzkrieg' is German for lightning war, which describes the idea of surprise and speed which was essential to the success of this new military strategy. The Germans had learned one lesson from the Great War of 1914–18: the tank was a war winning weapon. The tank's speed (up to 40kph) and power could make rapid advances possible.

Blitzkrieg took place in three stages. First, enemy headquarters and communication centres would be bombed by aircraft. Parachutists would be dropped behind enemy lines to cut telephone wires and destroy bridges. Secondly, the main attack would be carried out by tanks and infantry in trucks. This armoured spearhead would attack at the enemy's weakest point. The strongest points of the enemy lines would be encircled in the third stage by other troops following up behind the armoured spearhead. In the meantime, the main thrust of the attack, the tanks and motorised infantry, would continue driving their way through the surprised and demoralised enemy troops.

Compare the German and Allied strategies in the diagram below. What are the three most important differences, in your view? The Germans are in the grey vehicles and the Allies are in the green.

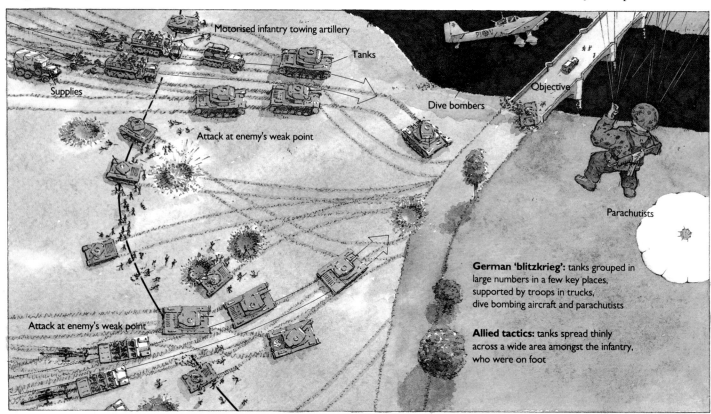

Motorised infantry towing artillery

Tanks

Supplies

Dive bombers

Objective

Attack at enemy's weak point

Parachutists

Attack at enemy's weak point

German 'blitzkrieg': tanks grouped in large numbers in a few key places, supported by troops in trucks, dive bombing aircraft and parachutists

Allied tactics: tanks spread thinly across a wide area amongst the infantry, who were on foot

⚙ The Allied strategy

The British and French High Commands, with a few exceptions, had failed to appreciate how devastating the combination of tank and air attack could be. They both preferred to use the tank as a weapon which *supported* the infantry as illustrated above. This meant spreading their tanks thinly across a wide area while the Germans chose to concentrate their tanks in large numbers in a few places. The technology of tank design had improved in several key areas since the First World War. They were four times as fast, much more reliable and had three or four times the thickness of steel armour-plating.

✠ The changing face of war

The generals expected the First World War to be a war of movement: troops advancing shoulder to shoulder across open fields, bayonets fixed. The generals were wrong. The Great War, as it was known then, was the opposite of a war of movement. The infantry spent four years facing each other from their deep trenches across 'no man's land'. Now and again, one side would launch a suicidal attack against the enemy trenches, wreathed in barbed wire. There were no dashing cavalry charges; the best use for horses was pulling heavy artillery and carrying shells

Source G
Information technology, 1916

Source F
A British Mark V tank, 1918. This tank had a top speed of 7 kph. It had a crew of eight and it communicated using carrier pigeons.

Source H
The British Matilda tank in the Second World War had a top speed of 25 kph, a crew of four and it communicated through its radio

and supplies through the mud.

Once the tank had been invented in 1916, it was used to support the attacks by infantry. Tanks had a maximum speed of 7 kph — about walking pace. They were not very reliable and often broke down. Aircraft were not used to attack enemy troops but for reconnaissance, eg to find out whether large numbers of men were marching to the front. This would mean attacks were being planned.

CHANGES: WARFARE FROM WORLD WAR ONE TO WORLD WAR TWO

1 Study the text and Sources F–H. Describe the ways in which the effectiveness and role of tanks changed from the First World War to the Second World War.

2* 'Both sides not only had better tanks in 1940 than they did in the First World War, but they used them more effectively too.' Explain why you agree or disagree with this view.

⚔ The end of the Phoney War

The period from the defeat of Poland in September 1939 to the German attack on neutral Norway in April 1940 is known as the 'Phoney War'. During these six months there was no fighting on land between the Anglo-French armies and their German enemies. To most civilians it seemed there was no war going on at all – although there were several bitter battles fought at sea. There were other humorous terms used to describe this period: 'Sitzkrieg' (sitting war) and 'Bore War'.

In April 1940, 'Sitzkrieg' once again became 'Blitzkrieg' as German troops invaded and occupied Norway. Norway was vital to Germany since Norway and Sweden provided more than half of Germany's iron ore. This was essential for the production of weapons. In addition, Swedish supplies had to come through Norway for six months of the year when their ports were frozen. Norway – despite some British and French help – was soon defeated. Not only had the Germans guaranteed their vital iron ore supplies, but they could now use the Norwegian fjords as ideal bases for their submarines (U-boats).

Prime Minister Churchill

Chamberlain had considered occupying Norway before Hitler to cut off Germany's iron ore supplies, but he hesitated. Churchill recommended going ahead with the plan, but Chamberlain was worried about world opinion if Britain did attack a neutral country like Norway. Hitler seized his chance. Chamberlain had miscalculated. His rather weak leadership was not popular with the public. Churchill, on the other hand, had plenty of fighting spirit. He had been an opponent of Hitler long before the war and had urged Britain to build up her armed forces. In May 1940 Parliament voted Churchill in as Prime Minister.

'The iron comes back.' The Norwegians had willingly sold their iron ore to Nazi Germany since the beginning of the war. Low's bitter comment reveals the price they paid as German tanks invade.

THE PHONEY WAR

1   Why were the Poles bitterly disappointed by the role of their British and French allies?

2   Why do you think Blitzkrieg was so successful?

3   How had the role of aircraft changed between the two world wars?

4   Explain why each of the phrases 'Phoney War', 'Sitzkrieg' and 'Bore War' were used to describe the period from the fall of Poland to the invasion of Norway.

5   Why do you think Parliament voted for Winston Churchill to become Britain's new Prime Minister in place of Chamberlain?

On 10 May 1940 Hitler ordered the invasion of Luxembourg, Holland and Belgium. Two days later, German troops crossed the border into France. The French were taken by surprise because the German tanks had found a way through the Ardennes forest (see map on page 30). They had thought that tanks could not pass through the forest and so only had second rate troops to defend it. The French were forced to retreat right from the start of Hitler's new Blitzkrieg.

A fort on the Maginot Line. Why do you think the French were so confident about its ability to defend France?

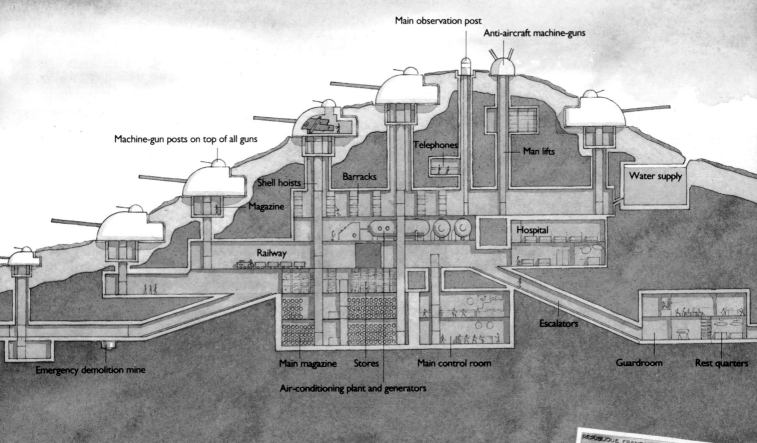

Main observation post

Anti-aircraft machine-guns

Machine-gun posts on top of all guns

Telephones

Man lifts

Water supply

Shell hoists

Barracks

Magazine

Hospital

Railway

Escalators

Emergency demolition mine

Main magazine   Stores   Main control room

Guardroom   Rest quarters

Air-conditioning plant and generators

The Maginot Line

The French High Command had been certain that the Germans would attack along the French-German border and between 1929 and 1934 they had built a series of underground forts along that border, known as the Maginot Line. France therefore gave little consideration to developing other plans in case the Germans attacked elsewhere.

These forts of the Maginot Line were impressive structures and the French were confident they could hold off the Germans. They may well have done – had the Germans chosen to attack them. A glance at the map on page 30 will reveal that the German attack on 12 May came at precisely the point where the Maginot line ended – at Sedan. The Maginot Line proved to be both expensive and useless, and the 30 French divisions that manned it were badly needed elsewhere. Had the French High Command used their excellent tanks in the same way as the Germans, the outcome may have been different. Instead, they spread their tanks thinly over a wide area and they were easily destroyed.

A French army recruitment poster from 1938, showing soldiers in a Maginot Line fortification

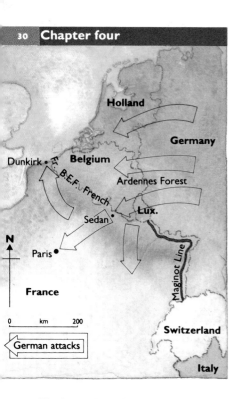

Blitzkrieg, May 1940

The race to the Channel: Dunkirk

The German tank commander, Guderian, now planned to race directly to the Channel ports and seize them. If the Germans controlled these, the British Expeditionary Force (BEF) would be unable to escape to England. The 380,000 British and French troops, who had been fighting in Belgium and north-eastern France, fell back to Dunkirk towards the end of May. There the Germans surrounded them. For nine days between 27 May and 4 June, the German Luftwaffe (air force) pounded the beaches as the Royal Navy ferried the men back to England. While this was going on, 40,000 French troops held the Germans off.

Around 340,000 soldiers were rescued from under the noses of the Germans. Of these, 225,000 were British and the rest French. In this respect, 'Operation Dynamo' was something of a 'miracle', but the British had been forced to abandon huge amounts of valuable military equipment – 475 tanks, 1000 heavy guns and 400 anti-tank guns. Some 68,000 men of the BEF had been killed or taken prisoner in the battle for France. The 40,000 Frenchmen who held back the enemy were taken prisoner.

Source J

When the first groups of the British Expeditionary Force reached Dunkirk on May 27–28 some of the troops lost their discipline. Armed British naval men had to restore control. Officers also abandoned their men in their rush to get to the boats. General Alexander was shocked at the behaviour of the British troops. On their arrival home in England some troops had such poor morale that 'they threw their rifles and equipment out of the railway carriage windows' ... The Ministry of Information told journalists to blame the defeat on French cowardice, while the BEF remained 'undefeated'.

(Adapted from Peter Neville, article in *Modern History Review*, 1991)

The British press and radio spoke of the miracle of Dunkirk, but the fact was the BEF had been driven out of France and Belgium in a serious defeat. Churchill tried to give a more accurate picture of events: Dunkirk was not a victory – 'Wars are not won by evacuations'. Reynaud, the French Prime Minister, desperately appealed to Churchill to send over ten squadrons of fighters (120 planes) to continue with the war. Churchill reluctantly refused. Britain would now need all her aircraft to defend herself. In Churchill's view the battle for France was over and the battle for Britain was about to begin.

Source I

The Daily Sketch, 31 May 1940

DIFFERENT VIEWS: DUNKIRK

1   In what ways is the account of Source J different from that of Source I?

2   Which of these two accounts would be of most use to an historian studying the evacuation of Dunkirk? Explain your answer.

3*   Source I is a popular and heroic view of the evacuation of Dunkirk and is still believed by many in Britain today. Why do you think it is so different from the view in Source J?

The surrender of France

It was only a matter of time before the rest of the French army collapsed under the stunning force of the German blitzkrieg. Some important French politicians, like Marshal Pétain, hated their own government more than they hated the Nazis and so France was a divided nation. Paris was occupied on 14 June. On 22 June the French surrendered to the Germans in the same railway carriage in which the Germans had surrendered to the French in 1918. Hitler had his revenge for that shame and the carriage, preserved by the French since 1918 as a memorial to their First World War victory, was now blown up on Hitler's orders.

Vichy France

Reynaud, the French Prime Minister, resigned rather than surrender. The new Prime Minister, Pétain, was willing to co-operate with the Nazis. The Germans took control of northern France but allowed the bulk of southern and south-eastern France to be governed by Pétain from the town of Vichy. Vichy France, as this area was known, was despised by the British and some French because of its willingness to work with the Nazis. The Vichy government in its turn believed the British had deliberately abandoned the 40,000 French troops at Dunkirk. What happened next would stun the world and enrage supporters of Vichy France.

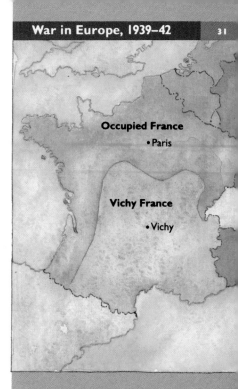

Occupied France
• Paris

Vichy France
• Vichy

German/Vichy areas of occupied France

THE FALL OF FRANCE

1 Why were the Allies surprised by the German attack through the Ardennes?
2 Why did the Maginot Line prove to be a failure in 1940?
3 What did Churchill mean by the phrase 'Wars are not won by evacuations'?
4 Why do you think Churchill was anxious not to exaggerate the 'success' of the evacuation at Dunkirk?
5 Read the section below and write a 25-line newspaper article explaining to your readers why the attack on the French fleet was regrettable but necessary.

✠ The British attack at Mers el Kebir

Churchill was determined to make sure that none of Vichy France's four fine battleships were seized by the Germans. If the Germans captured these ships they could control the Mediterranean Sea. The French fleet was anchored at Mers el Kebir, on the coast of French Algeria. Its admiral, Darlan, was given two choices by the British. He could either sail his ships to a British port where they could join the Free French forces and help the fight against Germany, or he could order his men to sink their own ships to stop the Germans capturing them. If the French did not make one of these choices, the British fleet would sink their ships for them.

The French admiral promised the British admiral, Somerville, that the ships would never fall into German hands. However, he would not accept either of the choices offered to him. At 17.55 on 3 July 1940 Somerville ordered his ships to open fire on their former allies. In the next nine minutes, 1300 French sailors were killed and three of their battleships were put out of action. Churchill had proved to the world that Britain would stop at nothing to carry on with the war – even sinking the ships of a country which two weeks earlier had been Britain's only ally.

In November 1942 the Germans did try to seize control of the rest of the Vichy French fleet. Admiral Darlan gave orders for his men to sink their own ships to prevent the Germans capturing them. Over 50 ships were sunk. Darlan had kept his promise.

DAKAR · MERS EL · KEBIR

The attack on the French fleet made it much easier for the Vichy government to stir up anti-British feelings. The poster shows Churchill smugly gazing at the ruins of the French fleet.

I haved helped the Norwegians...

...the Dutch and the Belgians also...

...and I particularly helped the French!

But now who is going to help me?

The Germans were confident of victory by the summer of 1940. John Bull, the symbol of Britain, was mocked in this German propaganda postcard.

CAUSES: WHY DID FRANCE FALL?

The following is a list of three possible reasons for the rapid defeat of France in June 1940. These reasons have to be put into the categories shown in the chart below.

- Some leading French politicians despised their own government and were prepared to support the Nazis.
- French steel output was only one third of that of Germany.
- The Maginot Line made the French over-confident about their defences.

(Remember how to distinguish between long- and short-term factors. Long-term factors make sure that an event – the Fall of France, in this case – will happen sooner or later. But short-term factors decide *when* that event will take place.)

1 Copy the chart into your file and then write each of the three reasons into a space on the left.
2 Put a tick into one of Columns A, B and C and another tick into either D or E. One of the reasons has already been done as an example.
3* Now find three more reasons of your own from the text and copy them into the grid, ticking the right columns for each reason.
4* Pick any two of the six reasons in your chart. Would events in 1940 have turned out differently if these factors had not existed? Explain your answer. (For example, what might have happened in 1940 if the French had never built their Maginot Line – would French military strategy have been any different?)

Causes of the fall of France	A Political	B Military	C Economic	D Long-term	E Short-term
1					
2					
3 The Maginot Line made the French over confident about their defences.		✓		✓	
4					
5					
6					

⚔ The Battle of Britain

Before Hitler could launch an invasion of Britain, he had to gain control of the skies by destroying the Royal Air Force. Any attempt to send soldiers across the Channel in vulnerable troop-carrying vessels would be impossible if the RAF still operated. The Battle of Britain was an air battle between the Luftwaffe (the German air force) and the RAF's fighter squadrons. If the RAF lost, an invasion of Britain would certainly follow.

Radar masts were essential for Britain's defence and very difficult to destroy from the air

The war in the skies

During most of August 1940, Goering, the commander of the Luftwaffe, sent his bombers to attack RAF fighter bases close to the coast and the radar stations. Radar was vital to Britain's defence since it gave the RAF warning of German attacks; it told them the direction in which the enemy were heading and the numbers of aircraft involved. With this crucial information, RAF Fighter Command could simply send up Spitfires and Hurricanes from the nearest airfield to intercept them.

The problem with bombing radar stations was that almost everything was underground. All that was visible were the radar masts and these were very difficult to hit from the air. Goering soon lost patience with this tactic and switched to bombing airfields further inland and factories making fighter planes. These tactics lasted from 24 August to 6 September and were proving very effective. Planes cannot take off from bombed runways and lost planes cannot be replaced if the factories cannot make them. All Goering needed was the patience to carry on with this tactic and the RAF would eventually have been defeated.

Lloyd-George (top) and Chamberlain (above) both considered making peace with Germany in the summer of 1940. Churchill (below) did not.

7 September: the turning point

On 7 September the Luftwaffe suddenly changed tactics. In the late afternoon, 300 bombers escorted by 600 fighter planes made their way over London. The fires caused by the raid became a flaming beacon for another 450 bombers that came that night. The raid over London was partly in revenge for British raids over Berlin in late August.

The 'Blitz' had begun and German raids continued every night or day until 3 November. During the course of the whole war about 60,000 British civilians were killed by raids. (It is worth remembering that British and American raids over German cities during the course of the war killed some 600,000 German civilians.) The Blitz was certainly a terrible ordeal for the people of London and other British cities bombed by the Luftwaffe, but it also meant survival for the RAF. While the Luftwaffe was bombing cities, the RAF was repairing its airfields and the factories were able to replace lost aircraft.

Goering promised Hitler that the RAF was finished. On 15 September Goering launched what he thought would be the knock-out blow against London. In day and night raids 410 bombers struck at British cities, but 60 German aircraft from the daylight raid alone were shot down. (The RAF, at the time, claimed to have shot down 185.) Clearly the RAF was not finished. Two days later, Hitler postponed indefinitely the invasion of Britain – although the British, of course, did not know that.

Some leading British politicians, like Chamberlain and Lloyd George, had seriously thought about negotiating a treaty with Hitler, but Churchill had refused to consider it. Britain had achieved one vital thing: she had stayed in the war. The American President, Roosevelt, now decided that Britain was worth backing and greater US military help was promised.

Source K

The German excuse that the raids on London are reprisals for British raids on non-military targets in Berlin is completely false. Our attacks have in no case been directed at civilian targets. The reports of pilots bringing back their bombs because bad weather conditions prevented them from finding their targets make this clear.

(Adapted from *The Spectator*, 13 September 1940)

Source L

The Times of 28 August [1940] described this raid [on Berlin] not as a reprisal but as an attack on 'clearly defined military objectives which had been selected a long time before'.

But this does not tally [agree] with the official account, written by Squadron-Leader Russell J Oxley, who led the raid. Unable to identify his target, Oxley made an important decision: 'I could have brought my bombs back, of course, but I didn't. I left them in Berlin'.

(*The Independent on Sunday*, July 1990)

A Spitfire from 303 Squadron

EVIDENCE: BRITISH RAIDS OVER BERLIN

1 In what ways do Sources K and L give different versions of the RAF raids on Berlin?

2 Do you think Squadron-Leader Oxley's view would have been reported in the British press in September 1940? Explain your answer.

3 How does Source K point out one of the dangers for historians who rely only on a few primary sources for their accounts?

4* Why might Source K, even if it is unreliable, still be of value to an historian?

⚔ The war in North Africa

When war broke out in September 1939, Mussolini decided that Italy should stay out of the conflict. Italy clearly was not ready for a major war at this time. However, after Hitler's stunning series of victories in 1940, Mussolini thought that the war was effectively over and that Germany would win it. On 10 June 1940 Italy declared war on Britain and the nearly defeated France. Now Italy could have a share in the German victory, Mussolini thought.

Mussolini's plan was to expand Italy's empire in Africa by invading British Somaliland and Egypt. To achieve this, a large army of 240,000 was assembled in Italian Libya. The Italian navy would supply it across the Mediterranean.

Italian forces drove the outnumbered British from Somaliland and made some progress with their attack on Egypt. A British counter-attack, though, quickly drove the Italians back and British troops entered Libya. The Italian fleet, in the meantime, suffered a serious defeat in November 1940 and was unable to keep Italian forces in North Africa well supplied. It soon became obvious that the Italian army lacked both the equipment and training to achieve much against the British forces, even though these were much smaller.

The British and Italian empires in North Africa

Field Marshall Rommel (on the right). The war in North Africa has been described as an old-fashioned soldiers' war. There were few civilians to worry about and huge open spaces in which to manoeuvre. Rommel was an expert in this kind of war. He was linked to the plot to assassinate Hitler in July 1944. He committed suicide in October 1944.

Enter Rommel

In April 1941, Hitler decided that the Italians needed German help. General Rommel and four German divisions were sent to assist the crumbling Italian army against the British, who had now been joined by Australian and New Zealand forces. Rommel combined his troops with the Italians to form an effective force which at first won some stunning victories.

It was not until November 1942 that the British, under General Montgomery, were able to fight back with the necessary force. Montgomery assembled a force of 200,000 men and 1000 tanks which outnumbered the German-Italian army of 100,000 and 500 tanks by two to one. The British offensive at El Alamein gave Churchill his first real victory on land against Germany and made sure that the Axis powers would not get their hands on the vital oil supplies in the Middle East.

The German-Italian army was driven all the way into Tunisia where they were trapped and forced to surrender in May 1943. The war in North Africa was over. An invasion of Italy itself could now be planned.

1 In what ways do these sources give different views of the war?
2 Explain why these two views of the war are so different.
3 'Both of these sources are wartime propaganda and historians should not trust them'. Explain why you agree or disagree with this view.

Source N

Italian postcard, probably 1942. Japan, the figure on the left, joined the war on the side of Germany and Italy in December 1941.

Source M

Daily Mail cartoon, March 1941

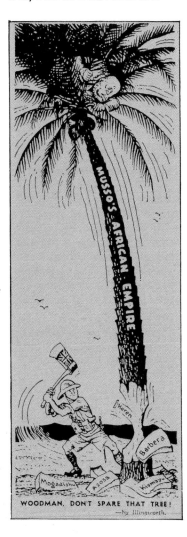

⚔ Conclusion

You should by now have plenty of evidence to fill in Box 1 of your hypothesis grid. You were asked on pages 23–24 to think of an hypothesis in answer to the question: 'Could the Axis powers have won the war in 1940?' You may have written that the Germans could have won the war or that they could not. The important point is to produce evidence from this chapter which supports or goes against your view. The key area to concentrate on is the Battle of Britain. If Britain had lost control of the skies in 1940 to the Luftwaffe, she would certainly have been invaded. How close to defeat was the RAF in the summer of 1940?

RAF pilots from 303 Squadron with one of their Spitfires

FROM BARBAROSSA TO BERLIN

⊕ Barbarossa delayed

By the end of 1940, it was clear that Britain was not yet beaten and an invasion had to be postponed. On the other hand, it was equally clear that Britain could do no real damage to Hitler. The list of countries under Nazi control was impressive – France, Belgium, Holland, Norway, Denmark and half of Poland. By the middle of 1941, Greece and Yugoslavia were added to the list. Romania, Bulgaria and Hungary were all occupied and forced to join the Axis.

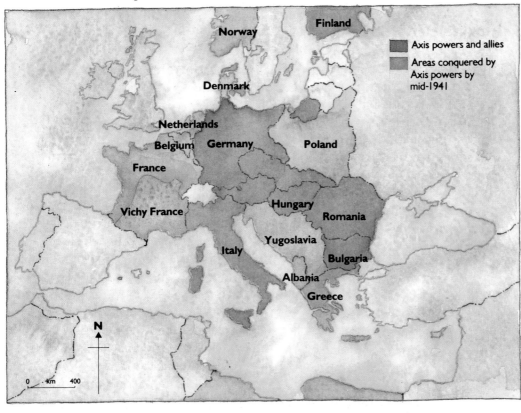

Axis powers and allies

Areas conquered by Axis powers by mid-1941

Europe, mid-1941

In the Second World War the red flag of the Soviet Union looked like this. The hammer and sickle emblem in the corner was the symbol of Soviet Communism. Today the Russian flag looks like this:

It took just three weeks to bring about the surrender of Yugoslavia (made up of Slovenia, Croatia, Bosnia and Serbia). However, this meant that Hitler had to postpone 'Operation Barbarossa' for five weeks. Barbarossa was Hitler's codename for the invasion of the Soviet Union – even though Germany and Russia were still allies. [The Soviet Union at this time was a vast nation and included today's independent states of Russia and the Ukraine. Most references in the text are to Russia since this was by far the biggest of the states which made up the Soviet Union.] Hitler had always loathed Communism, and Russia at that time was a Communist state. By destroying Russia he could wipe out the cause of the Communist 'virus'.

In addition, he could use the vast wheatfields of the Ukraine to feed his people and the important oil fields of the Caucasus to supply petrol for his tanks, planes and ships. Russia would be a valuable prize for his new Germany. The Russians, members of an 'inferior' Slav race, would become slave labour for the German 'master race' of Aryans (north Europeans). Hitler did not expect any problems. 'We have only to kick in the door and the whole rotten structure will come crashing down', he confidently told his generals.

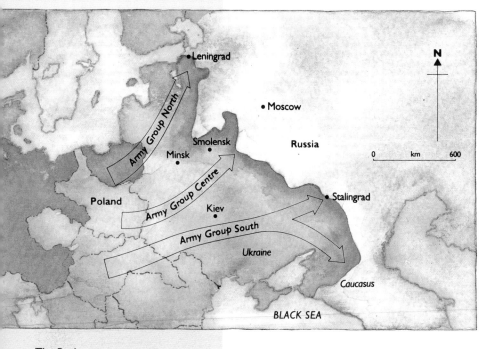

Source A

'Napoleon suffered defeat and so will the boasting Hitler', ran the caption to this Soviet poster which appeared in 1941. The shadowy figure in the background is Napoleon.

'Kicking in the door . . .

The German army of 3 million men, 3600 tanks and 1800 planes was hurled at the totally unprepared Russians on 22 June 1941. Stalin, the Russian dictator, had refused to believe British reports that Germany was about to invade his country. He placed his trust in the 'non-aggression' pact that Germany and the Soviet Union had signed in August 1939. The German forces were split into three Army Groups. Army Group North headed for Leningrad (now St Petersburg), Russia's second city and centre of her armaments industry. Army Group Centre made directly for the capital, Moscow. Army Group South's destinations were the Ukrainian wheatfields and then the oil of the Caucasus region.

The price which Russia had to pay for Stalin's misplaced trust quickly became clear: within three days almost the entire Soviet air force of 2000 planes had been destroyed. Churchill, an anti-Communist and strong opponent of Stalin, now welcomed the Soviet Union as an ally in the war against Hitler's Germany. By the middle of July, 400,000 Russians had been taken prisoner with the loss of Minsk and Smolensk. By October, Leningrad was under siege by the Germans. The siege of Leningrad was to last until January 1944. It cost the lives of 800,000 Leningraders who died from starvation, but the city was never captured.

Echoes of 1812

Hitler was sure he had learned an important lesson of history. When Napoleon's French army invaded Russia in 1812, the Russians simply retreated. As the Russians withdrew they 'scorched the earth', destroying villages, grain and livestock to deprive the French of shelter from the winter and food. The Russian army, although in retreat, remained strong and eventually counter-attacked when the French were exhausted, cold and hungry, deep inside Russian territory. Only 50,000 of Napoleon's army of half a million men survived the campaign.

Hitler decided that the Russians, this time, would not be allowed to retreat. They would be surrounded by his motorised infantry and tanks in huge 'battles of encirclement' before they could fall back. They would then be destroyed. In this way, the Soviet forces would have no army left to launch a counter-attack.

The Barbarossa campaign

1 Why do you think Sources A and B both refer back to the events of 1812?

2 How is Source C different from the other two?

3 Why do you think posters like Source C were needed?

4* Posters like Sources A and B were more common in Russia during the war than posters like Source C. What reasons can you give for this?

Generals 'December and January' to the rescue

The Germans got as close as 60 kilometres to Moscow, but a Russian counter-attack in December 1941 meant that they would advance no further. Despite capturing a staggering 3 million Russian prisoners by the end of 1941, the Germans had not captured either Leningrad or Moscow as planned. It was now that the significance of the delay in the launch of Barbarossa (because of the attack on Yugoslavia) became clear. Hitler had expected his campaign in Russia to be over *before* the Russian winter set in, but it was not. His troops were not ready for a winter war. Most had no winter clothing and thousands suffered from frostbite. Oil froze in the engines of tanks and trucks. The Russians, on the other hand, were well prepared for the weather.

Equally disastrous for the Germans was their underestimation of the size of the Russian army. They thought the Russians had 200 divisions (about 3 million men), but instead, they had 360 divisions (5.4 million men). No matter how many Russian armies the Germans destroyed or captured, there always seemed to be more to replace them.

Probably the most important factor of all was that Hitler had confidently expected to capture or at least destroy most of Russia's industries. This is because most of Russia's factories were located in the west of the country and this was quickly under German occupation. But Stalin had ordered 1500 factories to be moved as soon as the invasion took place. Ninety per cent of these were involved in weapons production, and they were now operating far from the reach of the Germans.

Source B

Soviet poster, 1942. The caption reads; 'May the example of our ancestors inspire you in this war.' In the background is a monument to '1812' and a portrait of the Russian general who fought against Napoleon.

The Germans (left) were told they would not need winter clothing. The Russians (top left) knew better.

Source C

Soviet poster, 1942. The caption reads: 'Follow this worker's example. Produce more for the front.' The heads in the middle of the flag are Stalin and Lenin.

VICTORY IN THE BALANCE

1 Why was Hitler so determined to invade the Soviet Union?
2 Can you suggest why each of the targets of the three German Army Groups was important?
3 Why did Hitler think he had learned an important 'lesson of history'?
4 What were the serious consequences for Germany of delaying the launch of Operation Barbarossa?
5 Why was Stalin's policy of moving Russian factories away from the fighting such a vital one?

Gaunt German prisoners at Stalingrad marching into captivity in 1943

The Russian T-34 tank was the best of the war. Its wide tracks made it more suitable to the Russian terrain than the German tanks. It was more rugged, easier to operate and its crew could be trained very quickly.

German Panzer Mark III. The German tanks, unlike the T-34, were highly engineered, sophisticated machines. On the well-made roads of western Europe they were very effective, but not on Russia's more primitive road system.

Stalingrad

The failure to capture Moscow before the beginning of winter was a setback for Hitler, but it would not have made much difference to the war. Even if Moscow had fallen, the Russians would have continued to fight – just as they had done in 1812 when Napoleon's army occupied the city.

In 1942 Hitler decided to concentrate his attack on the Caucasus oil fields. This would mean occupying Stalingrad as well. (See the map on page 38.) However, in trying to seize both Stalingrad and the oil fields, the Germans risked gaining neither. Army Group South would have to be split in two and so would be weakened. The battle for Stalingrad was fought from September 1942 to January 1943. The Russians fought ferociously to hold on to the city. It became a symbol of their defiance. It also became an obsession for Hitler and he recklessly threw away an army of 330,000 men in an effort to take it. On 31 January the German commander, von Paulus, disobeyed Hitler's order to fight to the death and surrendered what was left of his original army: just 91,000 troops.

Stalingrad was a turning point of the war in the East. The Caucasus oil fields escaped capture and the Germans were now desperately short of fuel. It was the Russians' first real victory of the war and it proved to them that the Germans could be defeated. The morale of the Russian troops – essential for any army – was dramatically boosted. From now on, the Germans were steadily driven back.

The end of the war in Russia

The Germans were only able to launch one more serious offensive against the Russians. This was at Kursk in July 1943. It was the biggest tank battle in history: 2700 German tanks faced 3600 Russian tanks and 2.2 million men were involved. The attack failed. The German armies, starved of reserves, were now forced to retreat rapidly and within twelve months of Kursk they had been driven from Russian territory altogether. From then on, the Russians drove into eastern Europe and headed for Berlin – the capital of Nazi Germany. At the same time, the British and Americans and their allies were attacking from the west and the south to link up with the Russians.

The price of victory

The Soviet Union paid a terrible price for their victory: 20 million soldiers and civilians perished in what the Russians call 'the Great Patriotic War'. By comparison, the military and civilian casualties of Britain and the United States *together* came to around 800,000. In the Soviet Union 25 million homes, 84,000 schools and 31,000 factories had been destroyed. The Communist government, which ruled the Soviet Union until 1991, always claimed that the West never gave the Soviet forces proper recognition for their crucial role in defeating Nazi Germany. In fact, 75 per cent of Germany's military might had been sent to the Eastern Front to fight the Soviet Union.

This Russian cartoon from 1944 shows a ragged general from the Russian front asking Hitler for orders. Hitler is shown talking through his backside!

Why did Barbarossa fail?

Column A: **Reason for defeat**	Column B: **Importance of the reason**
1 The Russians had a much bigger army than the Germans expected.	Hitler expected that his 'battles of encirclement' strategy would cut off and trap most of the Russian army. But Hitler miscalculated the size of the Soviet army. This meant they had more than enough men to counter-attack – even after hundreds of thousands had been captured in the first months of the war.
2 The Russians were able to move over 1500 factories away from the fighting.	
3 The Germans had not expected to be fighting during the winter of 1941/42.	
4 Hitler attacked too many different targets at the same time.	
5 The Russians fought with great patriotism to defend the Soviet Union.	
6 The German attack was delayed by five weeks.	

CAUSES AND CONSEQUENCES: WHY DID 'BARBAROSSA' FAIL?

1   In the chart above there are several reasons which help to explain Germany's defeat against the Soviet Union. Copy the chart into your book and fill in Column B. Here you have to say why each reason is important in explaining the German defeat. One of these has already been filled in for you.

2* 'Operation Barbarossa would have succeeded if the Germans had attacked five weeks earlier as planned'. Explain why you agree or disagree with this point of view.

The Italian campaign

The rebuilt abbey of Monte Cassino today. Its dominating position over the valley below can be clearly seen.

The war in Italy 1943–45

The German-Italian army in North Africa was forced to surrender in Tunisia in May 1943. This meant that an invasion of Italy itself could now take place. In July 1943, British and American forces landed in Sicily. By the middle of August they had captured the island from the Italian and German troops defending it. Mussolini was overthrown by the Italians themselves and secret negotiations began to take Italy out of the war.

On 8 September the new government of Italy announced its surrender to the Allies. The Germans reacted angrily to this act of 'betrayal' by its former Axis partner and fighting broke out between units of the Italian and German armies in Italy, Greece and Yugoslavia. The day after the surrender of Italy, US troops landed at Salerno. The US forces advanced along Italy's west coast and the British up the east coast, but progress was slow. Italy's mountains provided the German defenders with an ideal position to hold up the Allied advance.

Monte Cassino

The peaks around the town of Cassino, which overlooked the road to Rome, were controlled by the Germans. The town of Cassino was bombed to rubble by the Allies but the surrounding peaks were difficult to capture. The 600-year-old monastery of St Benedict stood on one of these peaks, Monte Cassino, overlooking the town. The Allies were convinced that the Germans were using the monastery as an observation post to spy on Allied troop movements in the valley below – though they could provide no proof that this was happening. The German commander denied that he had any men there.

On 15 February 1944, the Americans bombed the monastery, after dropping warning leaflets the day before to the monks and civilians inside. Nonetheless, 300 civilians died in the bombing. The Germans had not been using the monastery, but after the bombing they quickly set up positions inside what was left of the building. The bombing of such an old and sacred monastery immediately became a controversial issue. The Germans accused the Allies of barbaric behaviour. They, in turn, blamed the Germans for using the monastery for military purposes.

Source D

The bombing of the monastery on Monte Cassino was an act of stupidity against a sacred and historical monument. The Americans had no proof the Germans were using the monastery as an observation post – they just *assumed* they were. Once they had bombed it, the Germans, of course, were entitled to use it as part of their defences and the piles of rubble provided ideal cover for their troops. What is more, 300 civilians and monks sheltering in the monastery were killed in the attack. The bombing of the monastery simply made the capture of the position much *more* difficult.

Source E

The bombing of the monastery was regrettable but it was necessary. The Americans could hardly be expected to take the German commander's word that there were no Germans in the building. The ordinary Allied troops were convinced that the Germans had troops observing the valley and that these men were directing very accurate fire onto the American and British troops below. The Allied commanders could not be sure that there were no Germans there and so they *had* to bomb it.

Monte Cassino after the Allied bombing

THE BOMBING OF MONTE CASSINO

1. Using the views above and the text, explain why Monte Cassino was such an important military position.
2. Is it justifiable to destroy a work of art which cannot ever be replaced, such as an historical building, in order to help win a war? Give reasons for your answer.
3. Why do you think the Germans felt entitled to make military use of the ruins of the abbey?
4. Write a 25-line report to the Allied commander at Cassino, Lieutenant-General Freyberg, on the reasons for and against bombing the monastery.

Victory in Italy

The bombing of the monastery did not lead to an immediate breakthrough. It was not until the middle of May 1944 that the Germans' defensive line, the Gustav Line, was broken. The Allies then moved on quickly to capture Rome in June, but soon found themselves facing another German defensive position, the Gothic Line, running from coast to coast through Florence. Only in April 1945 did the Allies manage to break through the Gothic Line. The German forces in Italy surrendered at the end of April.

Mussolini had entered the war in June 1940 on Germany's side so that he could share in Hitler's victory. To achieve this, he told his generals, a 'few thousand' Italian dead would be needed. In the end, 330,000 Italian soldiers had died, together with 93,000 civilians. Instead of the promised victory, there was only defeat and destruction. One thing that the war did bring about for the Italians was the destruction of Fascism.

Mussolini's body is shown hanging from a garage in Milan after being shot by Italian partisans in April 1945. He had led Italy into a disastrous war and paid the price.

⬭ From Normandy to Berlin

The Second Front

Ever since the German invasion of his country in 1941, Stalin had been asking his western Allies, Britain and the United States, to launch an invasion by sea of German occupied France. The invasion of France, called at the time 'the Second Front', would force the Germans to transfer some of their 3 million troops from Russia to France. This would weaken the German forces and so help the Russians in their struggle to drive the Germans back.

Churchill agreed in principle with the idea of an attack on France, but insisted that the British and Americans first attack Italy. Churchill described Italy as the 'soft underbelly of the Axis' and argued that the Germans would have to take troops from France to stop the Allies' advance in Italy. The Italian campaign did, in fact, tie down 25 German divisions (about 400,000 troops). This would make the attack on France easier when it came because there would be fewer German troops in France.

Stalin was not pleased with this decision since it caused a long delay in the opening of the Second Front and meant that the Russians would continue to suffer terrible casualties. He suspected that Churchill and Roosevelt delayed the Second Front because of their hostility to the Soviet Union's Communist system. He thought they wanted to see his country weakened further before helping out with an attack on France.

This cartoon from September 1943 shows the sympathy of the British cartoonist, Low, for the Soviet view. The hard-pressed Russians need the 'Second Front now'.

Operation Overlord

From the beginning of 1944, plans were drawn up for the invasion of France. It was to be a remarkable project. It was vital that the Germans should not know where on the French coast the Allies planned to land. The Germans expected the landing to take place at Calais – it had a harbour big enough for the huge Allied supplies that would need to be landed and it was the closest point to the English coast. Eisenhower, the US general in overall command of 'Operation Overlord', encouraged the Germans to continue believing that Calais was the landing zone.

Three times as many bombs were dropped on Calais as were dropped on Normandy (where the attack did take place). Dummy military camps, complete with wooden tanks, were built in Kent, facing Calais. It was planned to put ashore six Allied divisions (three American, two British and one Canadian). Another three divisions would be dropped by parachute. The big problem would be keeping these men supplied and bringing on shore all the tanks, artillery and trucks which would be needed. The beaches of Normandy are too shallow to allow the supply ships to get close enough to the beach.

The Normandy beaches and landing areas

England

Calais
Hitler's main forces here

Belgium

Dieppe

Cherbourg

Le Havre

Utah
Omaha
Gold
Juno
Sword

N

France

Caen

Paris

St. Malo

Airborne landings

0   km   200

Mulberry harbours

The ingenious solution was to build an artificial harbour, called 'Mulberry'. Huge concrete blocks, called 'Phoenix', were towed across the Channel and then sunk in place by flooding them. These acted as a breakwater to ensure calm conditions inside the 'harbour'. Inside the artificial harbour created by Phoenix were floating docks on to which the vehicles were lifted. They were then driven to the beachhead on a flexible floating steel roadway. Within six days, an astonishing 330,000 men and 54,000 vehicles had been brought ashore. Within a month there were a million men in France facing just 400,000 German troops. Fuel was provided by PLUTO (Pipeline Under The Ocean), laid after D-Day.

The Mulberry harbour at Arromanches

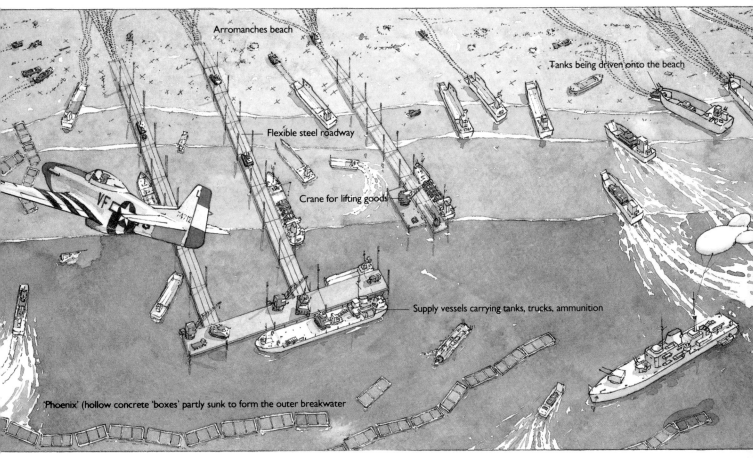

Arromanches beach

Tanks being driven onto the beach

Flexible steel roadway

Crane for lifting goods

Supply vessels carrying tanks, trucks, ammunition

'Phoenix' (hollow concrete 'boxes' partly sunk to form the outer breakwater

D-Day

Allied casualties were much lighter than feared – just 2500 were killed on 'D-Day', 6 June 1944. For one thing, the Germans were taken by surprise. They did not expect a landing in Normandy since they could not see how any troops could be kept supplied. Secondly, Hitler was convinced that the Normandy landings were not the real invasion and so he kept vital troops back in reserve, waiting for the 'real' attack to take place. This allowed the Allied troops to establish themselves on French soil. Thirdly, the Allies had total control of the skies and used this to bomb bridges and roads to stop the Germans bringing up reinforcements to the Normandy area.

The German infantry were bitter about the failure of the German Air Force to challenge the Allied aircraft. A popular German infantry joke of the time went like this: 'If the plane shows up dark in the sky, it's the RAF. If it shows up silvery, it's the US Air Force and if it doesn't show up at all, it's one of ours!'

German prisoners in Normandy in 1944

Russian troops captured Berlin in April 1945. Hitler promised a thousand years' of National Socialist rule. It had lasted just 12. This picture shows a Russian street sign set up in the ruins of Berlin.

On to Berlin!

On 25 August the Allied forces, led by General de Gaulle's Free French troops, liberated Paris from the Germans. The liberation of Belgium followed in September. Nonetheless, German resistance was still fierce. An attempt by the British in September to seize a vital bridge across the Rhine at Arnhem behind German lines went badly wrong. Of the 10,000 British paratroops dropped by air, only 2400 managed to escape death or capture by the Germans. In December 1944, Hitler launched the final German offensive of the war in the Ardennes, known as 'the Battle of the Bulge'. The offensive only succeeded in delaying the invasion of Germany by six weeks.

At the end of April 1945, Russian forces moving east met up with American forces moving west in Germany. Russian troops entered Berlin in the same month and on 30 April, Hitler shot himself. On 8 May Germany surrendered. The war in Europe was over.

OPENING THE SECOND FRONT

1 Why could the Soviet Union claim to have played the biggest role in defeating Germany?
2 Why did the Allies make such slow progress in their campaign in Italy?
3 Why was the opening of the Second Front so vital to the Russians?
4 Why did Churchill insist on an attack on Italy before invading Normandy?
5 Which of the three reasons given above for the success of the Normandy landings do you think was the most important? Explain your answer.

Other theatres of war

The bombing of Germany

The bombing of Germany's cities has caused a great deal of controversy among historians – and there were even protests in Britain during the war. Some objected to the bombing on moral grounds. Some 600,000 German civilians perished – most of them from 1942 onwards when Air Marshall Arthur Harris took over 'Bomber Command'.

The bombing method adopted by the British and American bombers was 'area bombing'. In 1942 US Air Force and RAF bombers dropped about 72,000 tonnes of bombs on Germany. In 1944 this reached 1.6 million tonnes. Area bombing meant whole sections of cities were identified and bombed to destruction and no effort was made to avoid residential or civilian areas. It was thought that this would break the morale of the civilian population, though German bombing of British cities in 1940 had clearly not achieved this.

The heavy bombing of German cities was also expected to destroy her industries, especially those crucial to her war effort, such as the aircraft and oil refining industries. In this way, the war could be brought to the heart of Germany at a time when she could not be reached on land.

Source F

A wave of terror spread from the suffering city [Hamburg] to the whole of Germany. In every large town people said, 'What happened to Hamburg yesterday can happen to us tomorrow'. Berlin was evacuated with signs of panic. After Hamburg among political and military leaders could be heard the words: 'The war is lost'.

(A German pilot describes the effects of the bombing of Hamburg, 29 July 1943, in which 40,000 died. Adapted from Adolf Galland, *The First and the Last*, 1955)

Source G

A German city after an Allied bombing raid

Darling, bist du mit deinem Bomber auch schon mal über Japan gewesen?
No — wieso, gibt's dort auch alte Kirchen?

The Germans were quick to accuse the RAF of barbarism: 'Darling, have you also been over Japan with your bombs?' He replies, 'No – why, do they have old churches there too?' The black barman in the background reflects Nazi concern with racial issues.

Source H

The bombing of Germany both by the British and ourselves had far less effect than was thought at the time. The German arms industry continued to expand its output until the autumn of 1944, in spite of the heaviest air attacks. Our attacks on their aircraft factories were a total failure. Strategic bombing was designed to destroy the industrial power of the enemy and the morale of its people. It did neither.

(Adapted from J.K. Galbraith, quoted in Studs Terkel, *The 'Good' War*, 1984)

Source I

On October 14, 1943, 291 Flying Fortresses set off to attack the greatest centre of German ball-bearing production. The Fortresses did severe damage but 60 were shot down. The strategic bombing offensive brought the German war economy almost to the point of complete collapse.

(Adapted from Brigadier Peter Young, *World War, 1939–1945*, 1966)

Source J

German aircraft production (British production is provided as a comparison)

	Germany	Britain
1939	8300	7900
1940	10200	15000
1941	11800	20100
1942	15400	23700
1943	24800	26300
1944	39800	26500
1945	7500	12000

Source K

German tank production	
1940	1500
1941	3500
1942	6000
1943	12000
1944	18000

NB Britain's tank production for 1944 was 5000

Source L

German oil production (tons)		
1944	May	662000
	June	422000
	December	260000
1945	March	80000

DIFFERENT VIEWS: THE BOMBING OF GERMANY

1 What do Sources J and K suggest about the Allied bombing offensive against Germany?

2 What does Source F suggest about the Allied bombing offensive?

3 What is the value of Source G to an historian studying the effectiveness of the bombing of Germany?

4* Which of the two historians' views above, Source H or I, is most clearly based on Sources F, G, J, K, and L?

A recruitment poster for the German U-boat service in 1942

U-boats proved deadly, especially in the 500 km of the mid-Atlantic known as the 'Black Cap'. Here convoys were out of range of destroyer and aircraft escorts. This photograph was taken from the conning tower of a U-boat.

Allied shipping losses in tonnage, 1940–44 (the greater the tonnage, the more ships sunk)

1940	4.0 million
1941	4.3 million
1942	7.8 million
1943	1.2 million
1944	0.5 million

The Battle of the Atlantic

Though doubts exist about how effective the bombing of Germany was in winning the war, there is no doubt as to the importance of the war at sea. Control of the sea was vital for both economic and strategic reasons. The side which controlled the sea could prevent essential supplies reaching the other side and this would starve the enemy into submission and force its war economy to grind to a halt. It was essential to control the sea in order to attack German occupied Europe. If the Allies had not controlled the Mediterranean and the Channel, they would not have been able to invade Sicily and Italy in 1943, nor land in Normandy.

The battle to control the Atlantic was crucial for Britain's survival since most of her food, weapons and oil came across the Atlantic. The Germans relied on their submarines (U-boats) to sink the merchant ships bringing these supplies to Britain. Unfortunately for the Germans, they had only 46 submarines at the start of the war and two years later they still had only 65. Hitler did not believe that a U-boat campaign against British merchant shipping could win the war. It is quite possible that if the Germans had been able to use a big enough U-boat fleet in 1940 and 1941 against Britain, they could have won the Battle of the Atlantic and forced Britain to surrender through starvation and lack of vital supplies.

However, when the Germans did have enough U-boats – 200 by 1943 – the British had the invaluable assistance of the United States to provide aircraft and naval escorts for their merchant convoys. The table on the left tells its own story of how the U-boat menace to Atlantic shipping was eventually beaten off to ensure Allied control of the seas.

☺ Conclusion: Could the Axis powers have won the war?

You have been investigating whether the Axis powers could have won the war at some stage. You should be able to find additional material in this chapter to add to your hypothesis grid (see page 23). The second theory in the grid refers to the possibility of the Axis powers still being able to win the war in 1941. At what point in 1941 did the Germans look as though they had won in Russia? Was there a chance that they might have won in the Atlantic in 1941 or 1942? What evidence can you find to support the last theory in the grid that from 1942 onwards the chance of an Axis victory was very remote?

THE WAR IN THE PACIFIC 1941–45

⩗ From European war to world war

Relations between Japan and the United States had become steadily worse since Japan invaded the Chinese territory of Manchuria in 1931. In 1937, they followed up this success with an invasion of the rest of China. Japan was clearly determined to carve out an empire for itself in South-East Asia.

For Japan such expansion was essential to become the dominant power of the region. Japan's most serious problem was a shortage of vital raw materials like oil and rubber (see page 16). The militarists* who ran Japan decided that the best way to acquire these was to conquer the countries that had them.

These militarists, the commanders of the army, navy and air force, also knew that this strategy was bound to lead them into conflict with the United States, the dominant Pacific power. In July 1941 President Roosevelt demanded the withdrawal of Japanese forces from China and blocked the sale of American oil to Japan. Great Britain, equally concerned about Japan's threat to its colonies* in the area, supported the stopping of oil sales to Japan. This oil embargo would have a devastating effect on Japan's military plans since the Japanese bought 80 per cent of their oil from the USA.

> **COLONY**
> A country under the rule of another, more powerful country; several colonies together form an empire (Britain had several colonies in the Far East)

> **MILITARIST**
> Someone who believes that military force is the best way for a country to achieve its political ambitions

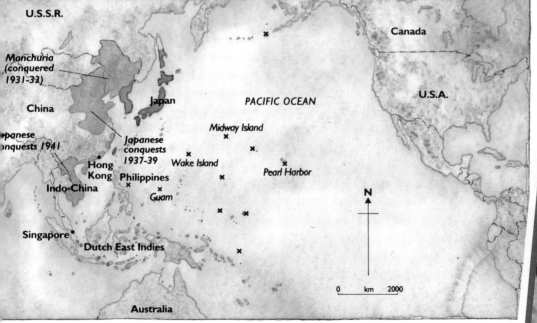

Japanese expansion in South-East Asia, 1931–41. The crosses on the map represent American military bases in the Pacific.

This '50th Anniversary Special' helped to make sure Americans did not forget Pearl Harbor. The Japanese preferred not to remember.

⩗ Pearl Harbor

The military leaders of Japan decided that they should strike immediately against the United States and seize the key areas of the region which produced raw materials, for example, British-owned Burma for its oil and Malaya for its rubber. The plan was to deliver such a crippling blow to the US Pacific fleet that the Americans would be forced to accept Japan's control of South-East Asia. It was decided that the Japanese fleet's aircraft carriers would launch their bombers against the US Pacific fleet's base at Pearl Harbor in Hawaii.

A complete victory – almost

At 0750 hours, early on Sunday morning 7 December 1941, the first wave of 214 Japanese aircraft struck at Pearl Harbor. No declaration of war had been made and the Americans were taken totally by surprise. An hour later, another wave of 170 bombers flew over to hit those few targets missed in the first attack.

The Japanese were pleased with their attack. They had sunk five US battleships, put another three out of action and destroyed over 200 aircraft. Some 2400 Americans had been killed. The Japanese lost just 29 of their 384 aircraft. Japan now had ten battleships in the Pacific to America's one. But when the planes returned, it soon became clear that none of the three US aircraft carriers had been at Pearl Harbor that morning. These had been the major target of the attack. Nor were the ship repair yards or the huge oil tanks damaged. The Japanese had severely damaged the US fleet, but not as badly as they had hoped.

Pearl Harbor: the turning point

The American people had been determined to stay out of Europe's war. They did not see it as any of their business, though their sympathies certainly were with Britain against Germany and Italy. Pearl Harbor meant that Japan was now at war with the USA and Britain since on the same day the Japanese attacked British bases as well. But the Americans were not at war with Germany or Italy and it is possible that Roosevelt would not have declared war on them. Roosevelt had proved himself a friend of Britain from the moment war began. The United States had lent and sold huge amounts of military equipment to Britain and he was anxious to prevent the destruction of democracy in Europe. Nonetheless, there was probably little enthusiasm in America for a war against Germany *and* Japan.

On 11 December, 1941, Hitler and Mussolini settled the matter by declaring war on the United States. The world's greatest industrial power was now fully involved in the struggle against the Axis dictatorships. Roosevelt quickly agreed with Churchill that the Allies should first concentrate on defeating Germany, even though Japan was clearly a much greater threat to the Americans.

This photo, taken from an attacking Japanese aircraft, shows how the US battleships were moored at Pearl Harbor. Why were they such an easy target?

The battleship USS California sinking after the attack

Source A

US intelligence knew the Japanese code and could follow every development in Japan. On November 29, the US Signal Corps translated a coded message in which an official of the Japanese embassy in Washington asked 'Tell me what Zero hour is'. The voice from Tokyo replied softly 'Zero hour is December 7 at Pearl Harbor'.

The Americans now knew that an attack was coming, when it would come, and where. US commanders in Hawaii and the Philippines were told '... an aggressive move by Japan is expected in the next few days'. The ranking admiral at Pearl Harbor decided to take no precautions. So officers and men were given their usual Saturday evening off on 6 December. Only 195 of the navy's 780 anti-aircraft guns in the harbour were manned. And most of them lacked ammunition. It had been returned to storage because it tended to 'get dusty'.

(Written by an American historian, William Manchester, adapted from *Goodbye Darkness*, 1979)

PEARL HARBOR

1   Look at Source C. Why do you think the Americans felt justified in showing the Japanese in this way.
2   Why do you think the US military leaders were so keen to hide the 'truth about Pearl Harbor' (Source B) from the American people?
3   The American military chiefs at the time of Pearl Harbor were *later* criticised for
    ● knowing about the attack and not doing anything (Source A), and
    ● trying to hide from the American people the truth about the damage caused by the attack (Source B). Which of these two 'mistakes' was likely to have the most important consequences for the United States during the war? (You can, if you like, argue that the consequences of both were equally important or equally unimportant. But you must back up your views with evidence.)

Source B

The American military chiefs immediately decided that the news of such a disaster would be unacceptable to the American people, and steps were taken to make sure that they did not learn about it. So effective were these measures that the truth about Pearl Harbor was still being concealed even after the war ended. The official reports claimed that only one 'old' battleship and a destroyer had been sunk and that heavy casualties had been inflicted on the Japanese. It cannot be argued that these lies were necessary to hide from the Japanese how much damage they had inflicted on the US Pacific Fleet. The Japanese knew exactly how much damage they had done. Reports in the Tokyo newspapers accurately gave the American losses.

(Written by a British historian, Phillip Knightley, adapted from *The First Casualty*, 1975)

Colliers
DECEMBER 12, 1942   TEN CENTS

DECEMBER 7, 1941

Source C

A US magazine cover on Pearl Harbor, a year after Pearl Harbor was bombed

PEARL HARBOR

1   How did the Japanese plan to solve their problem of lack of raw materials?
2   What made the Japanese decide to attack the United States as soon as possible and why?
3   The Japanese intended to attack the British in the Far East as well as the United States. Why do you think the Japanese were not very concerned about British military power at this time?
4   Give three reasons why the Japanese attack on Pearl Harbor was not a total success.
5   Why do you think that the attack on Pearl Harbor is described by historians as a turning point in the war?

The fall of Singapore

After Pearl Harbor the US could do nothing to halt the string of Japanese victories. By May 1942, the Japanese had taken Burma, Malaya, Singapore and Hong Kong from the British and the Philippines, and Guam and Wake Island from the Americans.

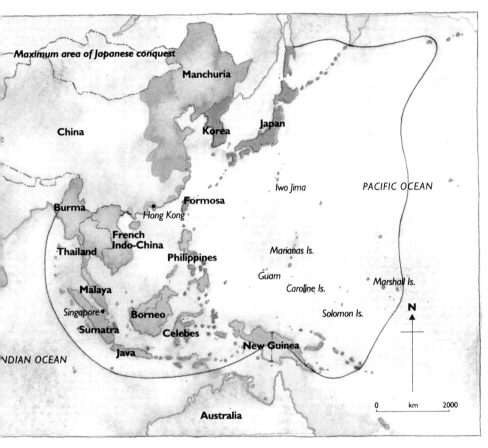

Japanese conquests in the Pacific, 1941–42

The loss of the naval base at Singapore was a shattering blow for Britain in February 1942. This came just two months after the sinking of the finest battleship in the Royal Navy, the *Prince of Wales*, by the Japanese in December 1941. The Singapore base was an island fortress, just off the southern coast of Malaya. Its huge guns faced out to sea and could not be turned around to face inland.

Tanks and bicycles ...

The British did not think it was possible for an attack to be launched across land, through the Malayan jungle, and so the guns needed only to face towards the sea. Neither did the defenders have tanks. Tanks, the British military believed, could not be used in the thick jungle and so were not needed. The Japanese had other ideas and came through the jungle with tanks and on bicycles. The big guns never fired a shot. Some 85,000 British, Australian and Indian troops were taken prisoner by a much smaller Japanese force of 30,000. It was the worst defeat in British military history.

The prosperity of war

Source D

The Depression ended with the war in Europe. The problem of making money disappeared. It became automatic ... People had defence jobs, money. We bought five hundred cases of canned pears from some outfit in Philly. At the time, they weren't rationed. They were terrible. The labels practically warned they were unfit for human consumption. By the time they were delivered, the government had announced they'd be rationed the following week. We were cleaned out of these awful pears in one day. The stuff just jumped off the shelves.

Before the war, competition was hard. You often ran an ad offering an item below cost to attract customers. You'd give things away. Now they were crowding in and taking whatever you had to offer. It didn't take a genius to make money during the war.

(From an interview by Studs Terkel, '*The Good War*', 1985)

Source E

1929 was pretty hard. I begged for a nickel to get something to eat ... I knocked on people's doors. They'd say 'what do you want?' 'I'll call the police.' And they'd put you in jail for vagrancy. When the war came, I was so glad when I got in the army. I knew I was safe. I had money comin'. I had food comin' and I had a lot of gang [friends] around me. I knew on the streets or hoboing, I might be killed anytime.'

(From an interview by Studs Terkel, *Hard Times*, 1970)

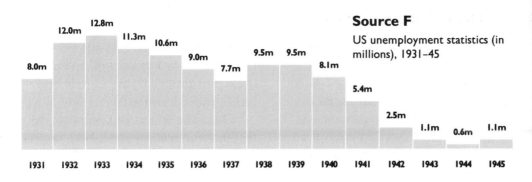

Source F

US unemployment statistics (in millions), 1931–45

1931	8.0m
1932	12.0m
1933	12.8m
1934	11.3m
1935	10.6m
1936	9.0m
1937	7.7m
1938	9.5m
1939	9.5m
1940	8.1m
1941	5.4m
1942	2.5m
1943	1.1m
1944	0.6m
1945	1.1m

CHANGES: THE PROSPERITY OF WAR

1* Using Sources D–G, show how the lives of some Americans changed as a result of America's entry into the war. What reasons can you give for these changes?

Source G

US plea for more output. American propaganda had to ensure that production did not slacken.

Cartoonists in 1943 had good reason to be hopeful about eventual victory. 'After heavy fighting we have established a very important base in the Pacific—Tokyo radio.'

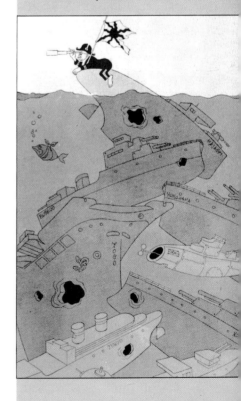

Midway – the turning point

El Alamein, as we have seen, was the turning point of the war in North Africa. The battle of Stalingrad was the turning point of the war in Russia (see page 40). A third great battle was also fought in 1942, this one in June — and at sea. Like the others, it was also a turning point since it put a stop to Japan's stream of victories and proved that they could be beaten. The battle of Midway was the first sea battle in history in which the opposing fleets never sighted each other. It was fought by aircraft launched from aircraft carriers. The Japanese lost four aircraft carriers, sunk by bombs and torpedoes dropped by American dive-bombers. The US fleet lost just one. Midway bought the United States valuable time to add new carriers to its fleet. Within nine months of Midway, the US had 19 carriers to Japan's 10. The Pacific war would be won by aircraft carriers and the United States had the industrial power to mass produce them quickly.

'Leap-frogging'

The British forces, based in India, planned to retake Burma from the Japanese but that attack did not start until 1944. In the meantime, the United States' navy and marines planned their campaign against Japan at sea. General MacArthur would attack from the south-eastern Pacific and Admiral Nimitz from the east. Both attacks aimed for the Philippines, captured by the Japanese early in 1942. In between the Philippines and the US forces were hundreds of small islands and the Japanese were prepared to defend every one of them to the death.

The Americans decided that some of these islands would have to be leap-frogged and left alone while others would have to be captured. Those islands which were attacked were ferociously defended by the Japanese. Iwo Jima, for example, was a tiny island just to the north of the Marianas Islands. You could walk from one end of it to the other in less than an hour. It was defended by 22,000 Japanese troops. It took a month of bitter fighting for the Americans to capture it in March 1945. Just 200 Japanese defenders were taken prisoner; the other 21,800 fought to the death.

⩗ The advance on Japan

In June 1944 the US occupied the Marianas Islands and now, for the first time, American bombers could launch constant raids on Japan itself. In December the Philippines were recaptured after the biggest sea battle in history at Leyte Gulf. Four more Japanese carriers were sunk despite the efforts of Japanese *kamikaze* pilots. These pilots packed their planes with explosives and flew straight at the US ships on suicide missions. The most important result of the capture of the Philippines was that the Japanese were now cut off from their oil supplies in the Dutch East Indies (now Indonesia).

Once the island of Okinawa fell to the Americans (June 1945), an invasion of Japan could take place. But it had taken four months to take the island and 13,000 US lives had been lost along with 130,000 Japanese. In Japan itself waited another 2 million troops, defending their homeland. How many more Americans would have to die before victory?

Truman as President

The US Air Force bombed Japan regularly. One fire bomb raid alone on Tokyo (a city mostly made of wooden buildings) in March 1945 killed 80,000 civilians in a huge firestorm. Yet Japan would not agree to the Allies' peace terms: immediate surrender without any negotiations ('unconditional surrender').

President Roosevelt died in April 1945. He had seen Germany defeated, but not Japan. The new president, Truman, believed an invasion of Japan would cost hundreds of thousands of American lives. Also, Truman did not trust the Russians as much as Roosevelt and he was worried about the spread of Communism in Europe and in the Far East. He wanted to end the war as quickly as possible to stop the further spread of Communism.

Tokyo was incinerated by fire bombs during a single raid

THE WAR IN THE PACIFIC

1 What two mistakes did the British make over the defence of Singapore?
2 Why was the battle of Midway so important?
3 What two pieces of evidence show the courage of the Japanese?
4 Why did Truman decide to drop the atomic bombs on Japan?

5 The atomic bomb dropped on Hiroshima killed the same number of people as the raid on Tokyo, yet most people only remember the attack on Hiroshima. Why?
6 Read page 55 and write a report of 25 lines for Truman outlining the debate over the use of the bomb and finish it with your recommendation.

Two bombs on Hiroshima and Nagasaki

Truman decided that the Americans would explode their secret weapon – the atomic bomb – on a Japanese city. Hiroshima was chosen and on 6 August 1945 one atomic bomb was dropped on the city. The bomb killed 80,000 civilians instantly and a further 80,000 would die from the effects of radiation. Three days later, another was dropped on Nagasaki, killing another 45,000 immediately. The Emperor Hirohito at last faced up to reality – Japan would have to surrender unconditionally or face total destruction. On 14 August, the Emperor announced the surrender of Japan. The Second World War was over.

Source H

A brother of mine had volunteered for an invasion of Japan. He was intensely patriotic. A couple of weeks after the defeat of Japan, he said, 'Now I know what you were working on. You saved my life. We figured', he said, 'on at least a million casualties.' I said, 'Yes, but it sticks in my throat, the two cities we bombed.' He said, 'Yes, it's terrible, but don't you realise what we were doing in Japan? We were all out fire bombing. We were trying to fry the Japanese alive in Tokyo.' In his view, the atomic bomb was no worse.

I still regret how it was done. I realise that a threat was not enough. It had to be dropped somewhere. But there were other places they could have dropped it without such a terrible loss of life. Of course, some people thought of it as a warning to the Soviet Union: We're not going to be allies any longer, so don't get ideas. We're stronger than you.'

(A scientist who helped to develop the bomb, from an interview in Studs Terkel, *The Good War*, 1984)

Source I

The success of the United States Navy [submarines] in denying Japan her vital oil supplies is told in one simple table of figures. Of what was produced in the southern oil fields that Japan had conquered, the following amounts reached Japan: in 1942, 40 per cent; in 1943, 15 per cent; in 1944, 5 per cent; in 1945, none. This was what really defeated Japan. With or without the atomic bomb ... Japan was finished, because her ships, aircraft, tanks, and vehicles could not move. They had no fuel.

(Philip Knightley, *Truth the first casualty*, 1975)

Source J

It was clear enough that Japan was beaten. But would she surrender without an invasion that would cost another 50,000 lives? The Japanese knew they were beaten but President Truman did not know they knew ... Hiroshima with its arsenal, harbour, factories and oil refineries was certainly 'a military target' by the standards of World War II. The dropping of the Hiroshima bomb was followed by a final demand to surrender, which was ignored. On August 9th a second bomb dropped on the port of Nagasaki, a city of 250,000 inhabitants. Unconditional surrender followed on August 14th.

(Adapted from Brigadier Peter Young, *World War, 1939–1945*, 1966)

Hiroshima was destroyed by an atomic bomb

Source K

Allied and Japanese military strength for the invasion of Kyushu (one of the four islands making up Japan), 1945

	Japan	Allies
Troops	2.3m	650,000
Aircraft	5,350	9,000
Aircraft carriers	None	20
Battleships	None	9
Cruisers	None	22
Destroyers	19	80

The four islands which make up Japan

WHY WERE THE BOMBS DROPPED?

1 Copy and fill in the chart at the top of page 56 on the issues concerning the use of the atomic bomb on Japan.

2 Look at Sources H and K and the text on this page. Which of the historians' views in Sources I and J do you think
   a was most popular at the time?
   b has made better use of the evidence?

The case for and against the use of the atomic bomb

Argument	Found in source	Whether the argument is for or against the use of the bomb
I The Japanese had a much bigger army defending Japan.	K	This supports the use of the atomic bombs since it proves that there would have been many more deaths (US and Japanese) if the Americans had been forced to invade Japan.
2 The Americans were worried by the threat of Communist Russia.		
3 The Japanese had practically no fuel left for their armed forces.		
4 The Japanese navy had ceased to exist by the time the bombs were dropped.		
5 The use of fire bombs in other US raids killed as many people as the bomb on Hiroshima.		
6 The bombs could have been dropped where they would not have caused so many deaths.		

⩟ Conclusion: Could the Axis powers have won the war?

An obvious piece of evidence to add to your hypothesis grid (see page 23) is the impact of the United States on the war. Did the entry of the US make an Axis victory more or less likely? Was there any point in 1942, or later, when the Japanese still might have won the war? What events during the war in the Pacific made the defeat of Japan more likely?

The question asked at the beginning of chapter 4 – 'Could the Axis powers have won the war?' – is difficult to answer. Could the Axis powers have won if they had not committed this or that mistake? What if the Germans had captured Moscow in 1941, or the Japanese had sunk the three US aircraft carriers at Pearl Harbor? Certainly, events would have turned out differently, but it is unlikely that differences like these could have changed the outcome of the war.

In 1942 the Soviet Union still managed to produce 10,000 more aircraft than Germany and Germany had to share her aircraft between three fronts. By 1945, the Russians had five times as many men and tanks and seventeen times as many planes as the Germans. On the Western Front, the British and American forces had 20 tanks and 25 aircraft for every one of the Germans'.

Japan faced similar odds in the Pacific. The United States built 86,000 planes in 1943 and the Japanese just 17,000. In 1944 the US built 44 new aircraft carriers. The Japanese had three times as many troops dealing with the Chinese as she had fighting the Americans. Perhaps, the question should have asked not whether the Axis forces could have won the war, but why they held out as long as they did.

THE CIVILIANS' WAR

Civilians had quite often found themselves involved in previous wars – especially civil wars. In the First World War civilians became part of the front line as Zeppelins (airships) and aircraft bombed several cities. This was a new and unwelcome experience for civilians in Britain. British civilians had become used to their wars being fought far away. The idea that they could become *casualties* of war came as a nasty shock. Nonetheless, the number of civilians killed in air raids and naval bombardment in Britain during the First World War was only about 500. The Second World War was to claim 66,000 in Britain alone and a staggering 30 million civilian lives across the world.

German bombers in the First World War dropped bombs over Britain which weighed 12 kg each

In the Second World War, the British Lancaster bomber dropped single bombs weighing 5500 kg. Clearly military technology had come a long way, but was it progress?

Pre-war attitudes

The Second World War had a tremendous impact on British society and permanently changed some aspects of life in the country. The Britain which existed before the Second World War was very traditional. Ordinary men and women accepted that running the country was best left in the hands of the traditional upper classes. It was accepted that the rich knew better and that working-class people should be content with what they had and not expect to mix with middle- and upper-class people.

Women were expected to stay at home and raise families. The most suitable type of work for women was in domestic service as maids. Some had professional jobs as teachers and civil servants, but women teachers, for example, had to give up their jobs once they got married. Few men, and probably only a few women, thought that women should be paid the same as men for doing the same job.

The war destroyed buildings and cities and shattered many lives. It also destroyed old ideas and attitudes and replaced them with new ones. This chapter and chapter 8 will look at what these new ideas were.

London burning, 1940

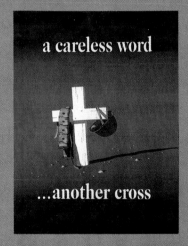

British poster

a careless word
...another cross

US poster. All sides in the war feared that enemy spies might overhear casual conversations about military matters such as troop movements involving sons and husbands. These two posters reveal very different approaches to the issue of 'careless talk'. Which do you think is more effective and why?

*INTERN
Imprison citizens of the countries Britain was at war with, such as Italians and Germans living in Britain

◎ **The Home Front**

Invasion precautions

After the Fall of France in June 1940, Britain faced Germany alone and expected an invasion to follow on swiftly. Preparations to meet this invasion were already well underway. Air Raid Precautions (ARP) had begun in 1938 and 100,000 air raid wardens and 60,000 auxiliary firemen had been recruited. Once war broke out a total blackout was imposed but road deaths doubled as cars without headlights ran people down. After 4000 people had been killed, a speed limit of 30 kph was introduced (but people had to guess their speed since dashboard lights were not to be used!)

German landing craft were expected at any time so areas within a 16-kilometre radius of the south and east coasts became security zones. Only people with permits could enter these zones and the beaches were wrapped in barbed wire. By 1 June, 5 million had been recruited into the Home Guard, consisting of those men between 17 and 65 not conscripted (conscription covered all fit males between the ages of 18 and 41).

'Saucepans or Spitfires' was the theme of the appeal to collect aluminium pots and pans to make Spitfires. They were not really needed as there was plenty of aluminium, but it made people feel they were directly helping the fight against Hitler.

Open fields were likely to be used as landing strips for German gliders so they were scattered with anti-glider obstacles — often derelict lorries, buses and even bedsteads! All signposts were removed along with street names — these might assist invading troops. Motorists were fined if they failed to immobilise their cars by removing a part of the car's electrics when they parked. These could have been used by German paratroops as transport (though it is hard to believe that they would also have carried with them the right ignition keys!)

The ringing of church bells was banned as this was to be the signal that the invasion had begun. Around 70,000 Germans, Austrians and later Italians (after Italy's declaration of war in June 1940) were arrested and interned* in camps — mostly on the Isle of Man. Most of the Germans and Austrians arrested were, in fact, Jewish refugees — unlikely allies of the Nazis. Suspected spies and traitors were thought to be everywhere and poster campaigns urged people not to discuss anything that might be of use to the enemy: 'Careless talk costs lives'.

Evacuation

At the very beginning of the war, 800,000 schoolchildren were evacuated from cities likely to be bombed along with 550,000 mothers and children under five. Many of these children came from poor inner city areas and were unused to the way of life of their often unwilling middle-class hosts in the countryside. By January 1940 most of these children had returned home as the expected air raids failed to take place.

In the summer of 1940, the evacuation of children began all over again as German air raids finally did arrive. For some of the 200,000 children evacuated from London and the south-east the experience was to last the next two years. The government published photographs of happy children meeting the pleasant new hosts who would take care of them for eight shillings a week (40p). The government slogan was 'Keep them happy, Keep them safe'.

Evacuees aboard a train. The government was keen to show this side of evacuation – happy children on their way to new homes. The reality was often different.

The reality was often very different and heart-breaking as the actor, Michael Caine, remembered (from Ben Wicks, *No Time to Wave Goodbye*, 1988)

'At first everyone was very nice and then the woman that had taken us there [the billeting officer] left and we sat down to eat. The woman said, "Here's your meal", and she gave us a tin of pilchards between the two of us and some bread and water. Now we'd been in this rich woman's house and so we said, "Where's the butter?" and we suddenly got a wallop round the head.

From then on it started ... not the husband, he was never there ... just her. What we later found out was that the woman hated kids and was doing it for the extra money. So that food was the cheapest meal you could dish up ... a tin of pilchards and dry bread'.

Michael Caine was evacuated for six years to Norfolk at the age of six. Not all of his experiences were as bad as the one he describes on the left.

The government wanted children to leave the cities to escape the expected German bombing. British mothers were reluctant to let their children go to the safety of the countryside into homes of total strangers. In many cases their fears were justified.

The country hosts of these poor, working-class children found it difficult to adjust to their different habits. The children were unused to sleeping in a bed and preferred to sleep underneath it. They did not know how to use a knife and fork. The strange surroundings and customs led to a lot of bed-wetting in the early weeks, as one young boy from east London remembers:

'The first morning after it happened we went to school as usual, but when we returned the door flew open and I was whisked into the front room where the mattress was drying in front of the fire. The lady of the house thrust my nose into the mattress and said, "How do you like that, you little pig?".'

One result of the evacuation process was that many people woke up to the poverty and poor standards of health that these children faced in their inner-city homes. Many had skin diseases, scabies and suffered from poor hygiene and a bad diet. Plans for a free, National Health Service were drawn up during the war and were put into effect shortly after the war ended.

Rationing

A generous rationing system was introduced in March 1940. Many of the British could remember rationing in the First World War and even welcomed it as a 'fair shares for all' system. In early 1941 when British merchant shipping losses were at their worst, rationing was more severe. Rationing meant essential goods were sold at controlled and affordable prices, while inessential, imported items like sugar were available only in limited quantities. Nettle tea was never a great success but it was more popular than acorn 'coffee'! Beer was not rationed but liberally dosed with water.

Sweets, of course, were rationed – a 250 g bar of chocolate or its equivalent a month was the allowance. Children's teeth and health, though, benefited. Indeed, the British were much healthier during the war than they had been before. Many nutrition experts believe that the wartime diet was better than that of the average Briton today. Some people believe that the changes which take place in history are changes for the better but change and progress are not always the same thing. Our diet certainly has changed from that of the 1940s but it is not a change for the better.

Rationing in force. This woman is buying underwear at Woolworths in June 1941, using her new ration book.

'INVASION IMMINENT ...'

1 How might signposts have been of use to German soldiers – particularly paratroops, dropped by plane?

2 Can you suggest why cities were 'blacked out' at night by having all lighting and lights switched off?

3 What evidence is there in the text that Britain was close to a state of panic in the summer of 1940?

4 Why was rationing willingly accepted by most Britons in 1940?

5 Far fewer children were evacuated in the summer of 1940 than had been evacuated at the very beginning of the war. Can you suggest why?

Workers at War

After Winston Churchill, the most powerful man in Britain was Ernest Bevin, the Minister of Labour. Bevin was a trade union leader before the war and was made Minister of Labour in May 1940 by Churchill. Churchill believed that only someone with Bevin's reputation as a fighter for workers' rights could persuade the trade unions to accept the changes which were needed to boost production.

Bevin used a mixture of threats and rewards. The Ministry of Labour had the right to make someone work in an industry which was short of workers, like the mines, for example. It banned strikes (though they still took place). On the other hand, workers were guaranteed a minimum wage and they could not be dismissed from their jobs unless the dismissal was approved by a tribunal. Workers were free to negotiate their wages with their employers.

Strikes

Patriotic appeals to boost production and make endless sacrifices had a limited effect. Some wartime workers did very well. Those employed in aircraft factories could earn up to £20 a week (£400 a week today) — at a time when the average industrial worker's wage was £6.50. But some workers resisted changes in their industries, especially the employment of unskilled workers to do skilled workers' jobs at unskilled rates of pay (known as 'dilution').

When power-riveting came in, requiring only one man instead of two, the shipbuilding unions insisted that a second man should still be employed beside each riveter. This extra man had nothing to do. Strikes in the shipbuilding industry were frequent, especially on Clydeside in Glasgow. In 1941

110,000 working days were lost in disputes in the Clyde shipyards alone. This figure could have meant that 110,000 workers, for example, went on strike for one day or 11000 workers went on strike for ten days.

Miners were also frequently involved in disputes with their private employers. Miners were poorly paid and were angered that some women aircraft workers were earning as much as £10 a week. The miners' union demanded £6 a week for their members. To try to achieve this, 220,000 miners went on 'unofficial' strike — that is, without the approval of their union. Workers remembered how their fathers had been treated after the First World War. Once that war was over, many found themselves without work; unemployment during the 1930s affected one in every five. The workers, this time, seemed determined to make the most of the fact that their skills were now much in demand because of the war.

"PUNCH," MARCH 10, 1915.

SOLDIERS ALL.

"TOMMY" (home from the Front, to disaffected Workman).
"WHAT'LD YOU THINK O' ME, MATE, IF I STRUCK FOR EXTRA PAY IN THE MIDDLE OF AN ACTION? WELL, THAT'S WHAT YOU'VE BEEN DOING."

Source A

A First World War cartoon from *Punch* magazine ('disaffected' means dissatisfied)

Underground stations provided safety from German bombers – at a price. People queued for a place on the platform. Conditions were smelly and there was no privacy and only buckets for toilets.

A woman welder during the war

Source B

It was frequently said that during the First World War the fact that people had to work together and all made sacrifices helped to break down the differences between the classes. In fact, for the civilian population the war increased rather than reduced hostility between the classes. Middle class people complained about the trade unions which were 'blackmailing the country'. They resented the workers who seemed to be getting rich.

(Adapted from T. Wilson, *The Myriad faces of War*, 1986)

Source C

[Frank Mayes at 17 got a job in an engineering factory making tin boxes for tanks. The conditions were bad and so he set up a union branch in the factory which 75 per cent of the workers joined].

When I came to work the next day the foreman, who was a typical bully type, said 'You're wanted downstairs in the office'. When I got down there the place was full of police. They said 'You know what we're here for, don't you?' I said, 'I suppose somebody's bike has been pinched'. And he said, 'No, it's not that'. He was a high ranking, three-pip fellow, and he said: 'You said yesterday – and I quote – "I would like to see Hitler in Buck-ingham Palace, the king shot, and the Nazis take over the country"'.' So I said 'You must be mad'. With that he slapped me in the face. Then he said, 'You get out now. You'll be charged tomorrow'.

(Jonathan Croall, *Don't You Know There's a War On?*, 1989)

Source D

While the poor descended to the tube tunnels, the well-connected and the well-off took to the big West End hotels, which had turned their basements into shelters. The Savoy was equipped with a doctor and a miniature hospital for first aid. It was at the Savoy that the only protest at the contrast between the ritzy rich and blitzed poor had been made. On September 14 1940, about 100 protesters from the Stepney Tenants Defence League . . . marched up the Strand to the hotel. The marchers arrived during an air raid and some made for the restaurant, where they sat down and demanded to be taken to the hotel shelter, as was their right. As luck would have it, the all-clear sounded almost immediately . . . The newspapers played down the story because it was Communist-led, while the Germans reported it as an anti-government riot. It is remarkable that there were not more like it.

(Peter Lewis, *A People's War*, 1985)

CHANGES: NEW ATTITUDES

1 Why were the middle classes in Source B so hostile to the workers and trade unions?

2 What do you think the real reason was for Frank Mayes being charged by the police (Source C)?

3 What point is the soldier making to the 'disaffected' (dissatisfied) worker in Source A?

4 Why do you think the author of Source D says that it was 'remarkable' that more protests like the one he describes did not take place during the war?

5* 'These sources show that Britain during the Second World War was a more united country than during the First World War'. What is your opinion of this view?

Women at work

Perhaps the biggest change brought about by the war affected women. Once again, just as in the First World War, they found they were much needed to help boost industrial production. By 1943, 7.5 million women were employed in war-related work – 600,000 worked as engineers, compared to just 100,000 in 1939. Unmarried women were actually conscripted by Bevin to do war work Most women were pleased to do so. Skilled work gave them a chance to prove their abilities and earn twice as much as they could in typically 'female' jobs, such as the textile industry. Nonetheless, though women were doing skilled work, they were only paid the rate for semi-skilled workers — if they were lucky. Despite this discrimination women were happy with their new jobs:

'*At first I was really shy — I had never worked with men before. But I became as interested in mending planes as I had been in dressmaking*'.

Women at war

Women also found themselves increasingly involved in military aspects of the war — much more than they had been in the First World War. Women joined the Auxiliary Territorial Service (ATS), the women's section of the army. One of the first things the army chiefs had to realise was that women wanted toilets with doors on! It was not very glamorous work — cooking, typing, driving — and ATS women were considered to be of a lower class than women in the Air Force or Navy.

Some did, however, get to work on anti-aircraft guns where they were allowed to do everything except actually fire them. Shooting down German planes was not considered to be suitable for women. But it was dangerous work — German planes at night would dive down the beam of the searchlight, firing their guns to put the light out. This cost the lives of 335 ATS members.

In the Women's Auxiliary Air Force they learned to operate barrage balloons and flew planes on non-combat missions. The least popular job for women was in the Women's Land Army — just as it had been in the First World War. Working in the fields and farms was considered smelly, hard and unfeminine. The pay was only £2.40 a week.

Women making aircraft dinghies

Barrage balloons. These air balloons were fixed to the ground by steel cables. The cables forced enemy bombers to fly high making their bombing less accurate.

Source E
ATS women working on a tank

Source F
This member of the Women's Royal Navy Service is shining officers' shoes. Another of her duties was to make their beds.

Source G
Working in the shipyards was hard and dangerous but women proved themselves more than capable

The not-so-weaker sex
Women turned their hands to a great many new tasks during the war and proved their capabilities, especially in jobs considered too difficult for the 'weaker' sex. Women took on jobs in shipyards, the docks and railway workshops. Hitler, on the other hand, was reluctant to recruit women to work in industry in large numbers. Nazi thinking only allowed German women a stereotyped role as carers for children and cookers of meals – not riveters and lathe operators. This attitude severely held back German production.

One woman was in no doubt about the benefits of the war:

'To be quite honest the war was the best thing that ever happened to us. My generation had been taught to do as we were told. At work you did exactly as your boss told you and you went home to do exactly what your husband told you. The war changed all that. The war made me stand on my own two feet.'

WOMEN AND THE WAR

I What do these sources suggest about the role women played in the war?

● Labour's election victory

In July 1945 Britain had its first election since 1935. Most people expected Churchill, the Prime Minister who led Britain to victory and leader of the Conservative Party, to win easily. Instead, Clement Atlee's Labour Party won a landslide victory, sweeping aside Churchill and his Conservatives. What were the reasons for this dramatic vote for change?

For one thing, the soldiers' votes ('the khaki vote') went overwhelmingly to Labour. They remembered the bitter lessons learned by their fathers in 1918. They had been promised then a 'land fit for heroes', homes and jobs. Instead they found that their sacrifice had earned them only the same unemployment and slums they had left in 1914. The new generation of soldiers in 1945 was determined that this would not happen again. They wanted the Britain which emerged after the Second World War to be different from the Britain of 1939. A vote for Labour seemed the best way to make sure this happened.

Churchill—out of touch

Labour promised a free and national health service and to nationalise the mines, railways, electricity and gas industries. The state would make sure that these vital industries would be run for the benefit of the nation and not just their private owners. Bevin promised 4 million new council homes — only 1 million had been built between 1919 and 1939. All this matched the mood of a people who wanted change and believed that Labour would deliver these promises. Churchill, a man from a wealthy aristocratic family, was seen as out of touch with the ordinary people.

Source H

Frank Mayes remembered how British sailors in Australia reacted to the news of Labour's 1945 election victory:

There were two or three officers there and a crowd of ordinary sailors, and the ticker tape said, 'It's now obvious that it's a Labour landslide', and a great cheer went up. And one of the officers said, 'Well, that's it. I'm not going back to England'. And a sailor said to him, 'Well, we won't bloody well miss you'. It was the only time I heard a private speak to an officer like that. It was a sign of the good times to come. We all thought that a fairer, new Britain was going to come about. Of course it didn't, and we were very soon disappointed.'

(Adapted from J. Croall, *Don't You Know There's a War On?*, 1989)

Source I

A wartime poster issued in 1942 by the Army Bureau of Current Affairs

Source J

This poster was issued in 1944 by the Army Bureau of Current Affairs. It shows a bright new health centre which would be built under the National Health Service. It would replace the disease-ridden slums shown behind it. The government withdrew the poster soon after its release.

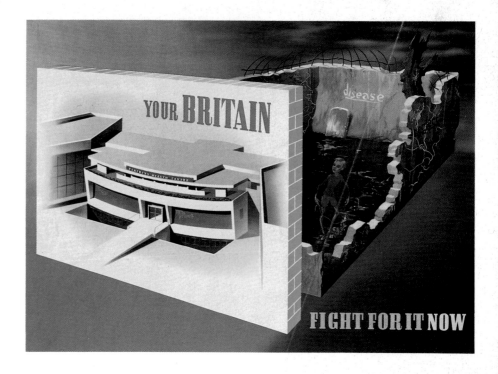

Source K

'The Last Enemy', June 1944.
Vicky, the cartoonist, made clear
his concern about what the end of
the war would bring.

Source L

Of the six million women in 1939 who
worked, two million were in domestic service. The rest were employed in low-paid
industries such as textiles, boots and shoes,
food and drink manufacturing or they had
lowly jobs in shops and offices. Few women
entered the professions and nearly all –
doctors, teachers, civil servants – had to give
up their jobs when they got married. It was
thought that marriage and motherhood was
the best career available. Home was considered to be a woman's proper place.

(Women before the war, adapted from Peter
Lewis, *A People's War*, 1985)

Source M

Many women who had enjoyed the freedom
of working outside the home now found their
jobs at an end or they were taken back by
men returning from the war. There was
pressure for women to return to their traditional role in the home and this was encouraged by the closure of many of the crèches,
day nurseries and nursery schools specially
set up to allow women to take war jobs. For
some women the new situation meant a
welcome return to family life, for others it
meant a sad loss of opportunity.'

(Women after the war, adapted from Jonathan
Croall, *Don't You Know There's a War On?*,
1989)

CHANGES: WHAT DID THE WAR CHANGE?

1   Both the posters (Sources I and J)
    were produced by the official Army
    Bureau of Current Affairs. Why do you
    think the government stopped Source J
    but not Source I?
2   How were women treated before the
    war, according to Source L?
3   What happened to women at the end
    of the war, according to Source M?

4   What was the cartoonist in Source K
    worried would happen once the war
    was over?
5   What sort of changes do you think
    Frank Mayes in Source H hoped would
    take place after the war was over?
6* How was Britain affected by the war
    according to these sources?

THE WORKERS' WAR

1   In what ways were women
    discriminated against before the War?
2   Why was Bevin a good choice as
    minister of labour?
3   Why did skilled workers object to
    'dilution'?
4   Why could it be said that the soldiers of
    1945 had learned the lesson of the First
    World War?

5   Some people believed that workers
    who went on strike during the war
    were unpatriotic and were helping the
    Germans. Do you agree?
6   Write an article of 25 lines for a
    newspaper explaining the reasons for
    the astonishing Labour victory in the
    1945 election.

Occupied Europe

'Massacre in Rome'

In March 1944 a group of Italian resistance fighters in Rome exploded a bomb in a dustbin as a German military police column marched past. It killed 33 of the military police. The Germans ordered the execution of ten Italians for every dead German. The Italians were driven in trucks to a remote spot outside Rome and led into some natural caves. In groups of five, the men were made to kneel and bow their heads. They were shot with a bullet in the back of the head. Not all of the Germans found this agreeable – some tried to get drunk to make it easier and they got careless. Many of the prisoners had to be finished off with rifle butts. After six hours it was all over and the caves were blown up, covering the bodies. Some of the relatives criticised the resistance group for the bombing and said they should have given themselves up to save the lives of the men. Six months later, when the Germans had abandoned Rome, the Italian authorities dug up the caves. They counted 335 bodies. The Germans had shot five too many.

Do you think the resistance group should have given themselves up to save the lives of the men shot by the Germans?

Hitler's headquarters after the July bomb plot failed. Hitler is showing Mussolini the damage.

'The July bomb plot'

By July 1944 a group of German army officers had decided that the war could not be won. These men knew that Hitler would have to be assassinated since he would never negotiate peace with the Allies. The plot was led by a 37-year-old aristocratic officer, Count Stauffenberg. He smuggled a bomb in a briefcase into a meeting of army leaders with Hitler. He placed the bomb next to Hitler under the large table around which the men stood and then left the meeting.

Unfortunately for the plotters (and the world), the briefcase was moved away from Hitler. It did explode and killed four officers but not Hitler. Stauffenberg was certain he was dead and put the conspiracy into operation. The plotters, having revealed themselves, were quickly arrested. Stauffenberg was executed by firing squad. Others were less lucky – they suffered an agonising death by hanging from meat hooks. Their deaths were filmed for Hitler to gloat over later.

◉ The Holocaust

Civilians on the British mainland never had to go through the ordeal of occupation by the enemy. Most of Europe was not so lucky. Civilians were regularly taken hostage by the Germans and shot as a reprisal for the activities of resistance groups. Whole villages were wiped out, such as Lidice in Czechoslovakia.

Of the 30 million civilians who died in the war, 6 million were Jews. These Jewish men, women, children, and babies were not the 'accidental' victims of bombing or street fighting but the victims of deliberate German policy. Hitler had always hated Jews and the 500,000 Jews in Germany in the 1930s had always been treated badly. By 1942, millions of Polish and Soviet Jews had fallen into Hitler's hands and he decided on the policy known as the 'Final Solution'.

This policy required the total destruction of the Jews of Europe. Along with 3 million Polish and 1.25 million Soviet Jews, 450,000

The aim of this poster about Lidice was to show Nazi brutality towards civilians

The Nazis forced all Jews under their control to wear a yellow Star of David, so that they could be identified

This poster is typical of Nazi anti-semitism. It shows the Nazi stereotype of the Jew as slave-driving businessman (the whip), grasping moneylender (coins in the hand) and Communist revolutionary (the country's outline is that of Communist Russia).

GROSSE POLITISCHE SCHAU IM BIBLIOTHEKSBAU DES DEUTSCHEN MUSEUMS

Jews from Hungary and 210,000 German Jews perished in the death camps. The 250,000 Jews who found themselves in the areas occupied by the Italian army in south-eastern France and Yugoslavia were, for a while, more fortunate. The Italians refused to hand them over to the Germans, but they were seized once Italy surrendered in 1943.

At Lodz in Poland, Jewish babies were thrown from a hospital window while an SS soldier below caught them on the point of his bayonet. These methods proved too slow and 'inefficient' for the SS. Eventually, in 1942, death camps such as Auschwitz and Maidenek were set up. Here Jewish men, women and children were told to undress and take a shower on arrival at the camp. Out of the shower came not water but cyanide gas. Death could take up to 15 minutes. The dead children and their mothers, still clinging to one another, were wrenched apart by the guards. The bodies were then burnt, after any gold teeth and hidden valuables had been removed.

An eyewitness

During the early stages of the Final Solution the Jews in the territories captured by the Germans were simply lined up in front of huge pits and shot in the back of the head by special execution squads of fanatical Nazis. One German engineer gave this account of such an occasion in the Ukraine (then part of the Soviet Union):

'Without screaming or weeping these people undressed, stood around in family groups, kissed each other, said farewells and waited for a sign from another SS man, who stood near the pit, also with a whip in his hand. During the 15 minutes that I stood near the pit I heard no complaint or plea for mercy.

'An old woman with snow white-hair was holding a one-year-old child in her arms and singing to it and tickling it. The child was cooing with delight. The parents were looking on with tears in their eyes. The father was holding the hand of a boy about ten years old and speaking to him softly; the boy was fighting his tears. The father pointed to the sky, stroked his head and seemed to explain something to him.

'I walked around the mound and found myself confronted by a tremendous grave ... Nearly all the people had blood running over their shoulders from their heads. Some of the people were still moving. The pit was already two-thirds full. I estimated that it contained about a thousand people. I looked for the man who did the shooting. He was an SS man ... his feet dangling in the pit. He had a tommy gun on his knees and was smoking a cigarette.

'The people, completely naked, went down some steps and clambered over the heads of the people lying there to the place to which the SS man directed them. They lay down in front of the dead or wounded people; some caressed those who were still alive and spoke to them in a low voice. Then I heard a series of shots. I looked into the pit and saw that the bodies were twitching or ... already motionless on top of the bodies that lay beneath them. Blood was running from their necks.'

A lesson of history

The Holocaust, the massacre of Europe's Jews during the war, is a terrible example of what happens when intolerance and racism are allowed to flourish inside a country. The worst atrocities committed by the Nazis took place during the war. The massacre in Rome in 1944 of 335 civilians is just one of hundreds of such incidents (see page 67). But the evil nature of Hitler's rule in Germany was clear well before the outbreak of war and so there was a moral element to the Second World War. It would be wrong to suggest that Britain went to war in 1939 *just* because Nazism was evil. Britain's interests were at stake and her empire threatened, but ridding the world of Nazism was a good cause and justified the war in moral terms.

Racism begins like this . . .

. . . and can end like that

There were also Germans who opposed Hitler — Communists, liberals and religious people. Many of them, like Colonel Count Stauffenberg, paid with their lives for this opposition (see page 67). There is nothing in the German character which makes them more likely to commit war crimes. Britain committed war crimes against the Boers in the Boer War (1899–1902) and created the world's first concentration camps in which 20,000 Boer men, women and children died. The United States committed war crimes against the Vietnamese during their role in the Vietnam War (1965–73).

The circumstances which allowed the hatred of Jews to develop in Germany in the 1930s and early 1940s could be repeated in another country at another time with another group as its victims. By making people aware of those circumstances and their consequences, future generations stand a better chance of making sure it does not happen again.

THE WORLD AT PEACE?

⭐ 'The Locomotive of History'

Leon Trotsky, one of the men who helped set up a Communist state in Russia, once wrote that war was 'the locomotive of history'. He meant by this that war speeded up the rate at which societies and situations changed. There is little doubt that the war changed a great many attitudes in Britain. Labour would not have won an election in 1940 if there had been one, but it did win in 1945. The Labour government then went on to bring in the tremendous changes referred to on pages 65 and 66.

The map of Europe was also transformed by the war. Russia (officially the Union of Soviet Socialist Republics or the Soviet Union) massively expanded its territory and influence in eastern Europe, and Germany was divided into two separate states for the next 45 years. A large wedge of east European countries were forced to adopt the same Communist system as Russia and the leaders of these countries took their orders from Stalin.

⭐ The new Europe

The Allied leaders, Roosevelt (USA), Churchill (Britain) and Stalin (Russia), met in February 1945 at Yalta in the Crimea (Russia) and discussed what to do once Germany had been beaten. At this time, relations between the Western democratic powers and Russia were still good and agreement was quickly reached.

'Here you are! Don't lose it again!' The Daily Mirror was anxious to make sure the peace-makers of 1945 did not make the same mistakes as those of 1919. The peace after the First World War only lasted 20 years.

'The last tribute', a cartoon by Low. President Roosevelt died three weeks before Germany's surrender. How does the cartoonist convey his respect and regret at Roosevelt's death?

The division of Germany, 1945. All the Allied powers were anxious to make sure that Germany would not be in a position to threaten the peace of Europe. How did the fate of Germany after the war ensure this?

The division of Berlin was similar to that of Germany as a whole

Treatment of Germany

Germany was to be divided into four zones of occupation – one each for Britain, the United States, France and Russia. Germany would also be forced to surrender some of its territory to Poland and Russia would acquire part of Poland. Berlin, though deep in the Russian zone, was also divided into four zones of occupation. The division of Germany was only supposed to be temporary but soon the West set up its own democratic state of West Germany and the Russians did the same in their sector, creating communist East Germany. This division was to last until 1990 when Germany was once again reunited as a democratic state.

When the Allies next met in July 1945 at Potsdam near Berlin, relations had become much cooler. For one thing, Roosevelt had died in April and his successor as president, Harry Truman, was more suspicious of Stalin and his intentions in Europe.

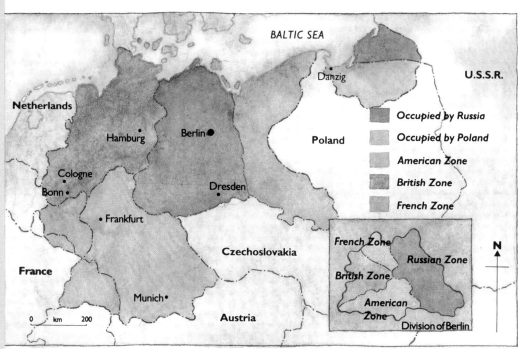

☆ The Cold War

There had always been tension between the Communist system of Russia and the Capitalist system* of the West. Before the war, this tension had never threatened world peace. The Russians were too weak and occupied with building up their own country. But in 1945, Russia emerged as the world's second most powerful state. Relations between the Western powers, such as the USA, Britain and France, and Communist Russia grew tense and frosty in the years following the end of the war. This 'Cold War' ('cold' because it was not a real, shooting or 'hot' war) dominated international relations for the next 45 years – until Russia abandoned its Communist system in 1991.

Soviet expansion

The Russian 'Red Army' had driven the Germans out of all of eastern Europe and the Russians had been welcomed as liberators from Nazi oppression by these countries. Unfortunately for the peoples of Poland, Czechoslovakia, Hungary, Romania, Bulgaria and eastern Germany, the Red Army had no intention of leaving. Instead, Communist dictatorships were set up in these states and the leaders of these governments took their orders from Stalin in Moscow. Churchill, in

Source A
Europe, 1939

Source B
Europe, 1949

a speech in 1946, referred to the countries under Russian control as being behind 'the Iron Curtain'. This was because the Communists set up barbed wire fences and observation towers to stop people leaving the areas they now controlled.

Stalin wanted to establish a ring of Communist 'satellite' states in eastern Europe in which the Red Army would be based. Russia had twice been invaded in 1914 and 1941. Now she had a protective ring of eastern European Communist states to act as a buffer against another invasion.

THE NEW EUROPE

1 Some independent states on the map in 1939 no longer existed in 1949. Which ones are they?

2 Which countries lost land and which gained land as a result of the war.

3 Can you suggest any reason why Stalin was keen to ensure that Poland gained territory at the expense of Germany?

4 List all the states which were now to the east of the Iron Curtain.

5 What did all these states now have in common?

6 Why was Berlin likely to be a cause of tension between the West and the Russians?

7 Do the maps suggest any reasons why the British and Americans were so concerned about Russian influence in Europe?

The Collapse of Communism in Europe

Though Russia was a huge country with tremendous natural resources, it did not have an efficient economic system. The Communist system could not feed its people properly, nor give them a good standard of living. In 1966, for example, there were only four refrigerators for every 100 Russians (compared to 30 for every 100 Americans). The problem was that in order to compete with the US the Russians were spending huge amounts of money they could not afford on the development of nuclear and conventional weapons.

In 1989, the Russian leader, Gorbachev, gave up Russian control of eastern Europe and these states quickly abandoned Communism. Two years later, Communism which had lasted 74 years, was also abandoned by the Russian people. The Soviet Union ceased to exist.

The failure of old-style Communists to regain control of the Soviet Union in August 1991 brought about the rapid break-up of Soviet Communism in Russia and the other republics of the Soviet Union. The Cold War was over.

★ The end of European power

The influence of the great European states like Britain and France had already started to weaken before 1939. The Second World War sped up this process of decline and the world after 1945 was to be dominated by just two super powers, the United States and Russia. However, neither Britain nor France realised this straight away. They continued to behave for another ten years or so as though they could still influence world events.

The war and the early defeats suffered by the British at the hands of the Japanese showed the peoples ruled by the British and French empires that the Europeans could be beaten. These peoples were not willing to welcome back their old colonial rulers. The Vietnamese fought the French and Britain faced rebellions in her African colonies. The Labour government quickly agreed to the independence of India in 1947.

THE COLD WAR

1. What happened to Germany after the war?
2. What was the 'Cold War' and why did it develop in Europe after 1945?
3. What brought the Cold War in Europe to an end?
4. Why did Stalin want to extend Russian control in Eastern Europe?
5. How did the war encourage the break-up of the empires of Britain and France?

★ The United Nations Organisation

The League of Nations organisation had disintegrated on the outbreak of war in 1939 and the Allies agreed that something more effective should replace it. The United Nations Organisation was set up in 1945. Its major purpose was to keep the peace in the world by encouraging economic and social progress throughout the world, especially in the poorer nations of what came to be known as the Third World.

Through the General Assembly, which meets every year, it provides a place where its member nations can discuss problems of all kinds. Proposals can be approved to deal with these problems. Every member has a vote in the General Assembly, no matter how small the country.

A UN Security Council meeting

However, the really powerful UN body is not the General Assembly but the Security Council. This consists of five permanent members and some elected ones. The permanent members are the Allies of the Second World War: the United States, Russia, China, Britain and France. Any proposal made by the Assembly or the Security Council can be vetoed (stopped) by a member of the Security Council.

The UN Charter sets out the rules and ideals of the organisation. In addition to maintaining world peace, the Charter also states its 'faith in fundamental human rights'. These include the right to free speech, the freedom to believe in any religion, the right to leave a country and the right to equal treatment for all races.

UN Agencies

The Charter set up a number of agencies to ensure that the world would be not just a safer place but also a better educated, more prosperous and healthier one. Prominent among these are UNESCO (the United Nations Educational, Scientific and Cultural Organisation), FAO (the Food and Agricultural Organisation) and WHO (the World Health Organisation). One UN agency came into being before the official founding of the UN. This was UNRRA (the United Nations Relief and Rehabilitation Administration).

UNRRA was set up by the Allies in 1943 to deal with the huge number of refugees and stateless people that were expected at the end of the war. In 1945 there were an estimated 21 million refugees – people trying to escape from the conflict, people with no homes or survivors from the concentration camps. They had to be housed, fed and returned to their homes – if they still existed. Some had fled to escape not just the fighting but also the spread of Soviet Communism and these people had to be found new homes elsewhere.

German refugees in 1945 search the ruined streets of Berlin for a place to stay

The UN since 1945

The United Nations has been a greater success than the pre-war League of Nations. For one thing, all the major world powers are members (unlike the League which the USA did not join). It brings together a large number of countries – 50 in 1945 and about 160 today.

The UN can also use military force and peace-keeping troops to ensure its policies are supported – something the League of Nations could never do. Much of the best work of the UN has been carried out quietly by the agencies in the field of health, agriculture and education.

★ Britain after the war

Britain played a major role in the Allied victory, though it was less important than either that of Russia, with her huge armed forces, or the United States, with her industrial resources. However, given that Britain is a much smaller country, the cost to Britain in terms of losses and expense was tremendous. Britain was bankrupted by the war and the first thing the new Labour government had to do was borrow £1 billion from the United States (though the British asked for £1.5 billion). Fortunately for Britain, the other states of Europe — Germany, France and Italy — were even more severely affected by the war and so Britain's weak economic state was not immediately obvious. Indeed, she managed to increase exports by 75 per cent from the 1939 figure. She developed her own atomic bomb in 1952, three years after the Russians, and until 1960 only the United States, Russia and Britain had this weapon.

'Switching the hunt.' There were thousands of foreign refugees in Britain in 1945. This cartoonist did not see them as a problem, but rather as a scapegoat for those who wanted someone to blame for Britain's difficulties. What other point is he making?

The Blitz had made 2 million people homeless. In 1946 only 51,000 new houses were built.

Source C

World manufacturing output. The graph measures British and US machine-made production as a percentage of world production. In 1880, for example, Britain made 23 per cent of all the goods made by machines in the world and was therefore the richest country in the world. It is a way of measuring a country's wealth – the bigger the percentage, the more prosperous the country.

Britain loses power

All this helped to conceal from the British people and the world that Britain was really no longer a great world power. From 1945 until the break-up of the Soviet Union in 1991 two countries were dominant: the United States and the Soviet Union (Russia). Britain, despite being on the winning side, had really lost a great deal as a result of the war. Within twenty years of the end of the war, the British Empire had been broken up and today Britain ranks as only the world's fifth richest nation – behind the United States, Japan, Germany and France.

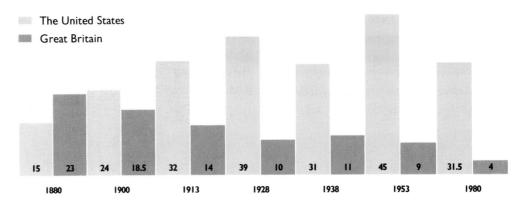

☐ The United States
■ Great Britain

| 15 | 23 | 24 | 18.5 | 32 | 14 | 39 | 10 | 31 | 11 | 45 | 9 | 31.5 | 4 |
| 1880 | | 1900 | | 1913 | | 1928 | | 1938 | | 1953 | | 1980 | |

WORLD MANUFACTURING OUTPUT

1 What does Source C suggest about Britain's economic performance since 1880?

2 Can you suggest any reason why Britain's share of world output fell by only two per cent between 1938 and 1953? (Clue: Britain's trading rivals)

3 Can you suggest any reason why the United States' share increased by so much during the same period?

4 Do these statistics prove that Britain was a poorer country in 1953 than she had been in 1880? Give reasons for your answer.

★ Conclusion

The Second World War shaped the history of the world for the next fifty years. It established a world dominated by just two global powers: the United States and Communist Russia. The tension which existed between these two nations, the 'Cold War', played a major part in world political affairs. Sometimes, this tension came close to bringing about a Third World War, especially in 1962 during the Cuban Missile Crisis.

Europe ceased to be the dominant continent and the two leading European powers, Britain and France, became no more than second-rank states. Germany and Japan, on the other hand, recovered quickly from defeat to become wealthy and advanced states. It seemed as though this would be the pattern for some time to come. However, the ending of Communism in eastern Europe and then in the Soviet Union itself brought about a sudden transformation of Europe at the beginning of the 1990s. Some of the changes which came about as a result of the war proved not to be permanent and the world may be a safer place as a result.

★ The people's war?

Many of those who lived through the war, however, speak with warmth about what they remember. The idea that everybody was in it together, that everyone, no matter what class they were, all had to work together for the common good left its mark. The following three extracts were taken from *The People's War* by Peter Lewis (1986):

'There was this general feeling that we were one nation — a feeling of equality, that everybody was valuable, that everybody's effort counted. It was a much more equal society than we had before and some of it remains.'

'There are a large number of people who will tell you that in spite of all the fear, the loss, the suffering and so on, the war years were the best years of their life. By and large we ate the same rations, we wore the same clothes and shared a common purpose.'

'It was a great community spirit. I wouldn't have missed it for the world. I went straight overseas for two or three years at the end of the war and when I came back, it had gone.'

It is an understandable feature of human nature that the bad memories are shut out. It is not only the memories of terrible deaths and injuries that are mercifully put aside

— these are expected in war. But the memories of looting, of people returning to their bombed out homes to find what remained of their furniture and valuables had been stolen — these too are shut out. There was a tremendous feeling of all being 'in it together', but there was also the anger of the East Enders who booed the King and Queen when they visited their bomb damaged streets. Such things did happen but they are largely forgotten. People sometimes only remember what they want to remember.

This cheerful family from South East London have survived a bomb explosion in their garden. It is interesting to note that the Churchillian 'V for Victory' sign is not to be seen in the photograph. Clearly Londoners preferred the traditional 'thumbs-up' symbol, even in an obviously staged photograph.

The other side of the blitz — one of the many who did not survive

Index

▥ Acknowledgements

The publishers would like to thank the following for permission to reproduce photographs:

E. T. Archive pages 13, 68t; Neil DeMarco page 42; Hulton Deutsch Collection pages 5, 8b, 11, 15, 18t, 20, 24, 34, 35, 36b, 40t, 43b, 47, 50, 54, 57tr & b, 59t, 60, 62, 67, 70r, 78t; Imperial War Museum pages 27, 31, 38, 39tl & r, 43t, 58br, 61, 64, 65; Magnum pages 16b, 37t, 40m, 45, 68bl 77; Network page 70l; Peter Newark pages 4, 6, 7t, 8t, 12, 14, 18, 19, 23, 25, 29, 33, 36t, 39br, 41, 48, 51, 53, 57, 58t & bl, 63b, 68br; Popperfoto page 39bl; Frank Spooner Pictures pages 37b, 74, 75; Süddeutscher Verlag page 7b; The Tank Museum page 40b; Time Inc. © copyright 1991 page 49; Topham Picture Source pages 22, 46, 55, 59b, 76, 79b.

Cartoons:

Associated Newspapers pages 36, 66, 77; Express Newspapers pages 6, 12, 15, 20, 28, 44, 72; Mirror Group Newspapers pages 53, 77; St Louis Post-Despatch page 19.

Cover: Peter Newark
Illustrations: Mike Hingley and Martin Sanders